**DEPARTMENT OF THE NAVY**
HEADQUARTERS UNITED STATES MARINE CORPS
3000 MARINE CORPS PENTAGON
WASHINGTON, D.C. 20350-3000

I0415692

# COMBAT CAMERA (COMCAM) TRAINING AND READINESS (T&R) MANUAL

**DEPARTMENT OF THE NAVY**
HEADQUARTERS UNITED STATES MARINE CORPS
3000 MARINE CORPS PENTAGON
WASHINGTON, D.C. 20350-3000

NAVMC 3500.77A
C 469
30 Jan 2012

NAVMC 3500.77A

From:   Commandant of the Marine Corps
To:     Distribution List

Subj:   COMBAT CAMERA (COMCAM) TRAINING AND READINESS (T&R) MANUAL

Ref:    (a) MCO P3500.72A
        (b) MCO 1553.3A
        (c) MCO 3400.3F
        (d) MCO 3500.27B W/Erratum
        (e) MCRP 3-0A
        (f) MCRP 3-0B
        (g) MCO 1553.2B

1. <u>Purpose</u>.  Per reference (a), this T&R Manual establishes training standards, regulations and policies regarding the training of Marines in the Combat Camera occupational field.

2. <u>Cancellation</u>.  NAVMC 3500.77

3. <u>Scope</u>

    a.  The Core Capability Mission Essential Task List (METL) in this Manual is used in Defense Readiness Reporting System (DRRS) for assessment and reporting of unit readiness.  Units achieve training readiness for reporting in DRRS by gaining and sustaining proficiency in the training events in this manual at both collective unit and individual levels.

    b.  Per reference (b), commanders will conduct an internal assessment of the unit's ability to execute its mission and develop long-, mid-, and short-range training plans to sustain proficiency and correct deficiencies. Training plans will incorporate these events to standardize training and provide objective assessment of progress toward attaining combat readiness. Commanders will keep records at the unit and individual levels to record training achievements, identify training gaps and document objective assessments of readiness associated with training Marines and assigned Navy personnel.  Commanders will use reference (c) to incorporate nuclear, biological and chemical defense training into training plans and reference (d) to integrate operational risk management.  References (e) and (f) provide amplifying information for effective planning and management of training within the unit.

    c.  Formal school and training detachment commanders will use references (a) and (g) to ensure programs of instruction meet skill training requirements established in this Manual and provides career-progression training in the events designated for initial training in the formal school environment.

4. _Information_. Commanding General (CG), Training and Education Command (TECOM) will update this T&R Manual as necessary to provide current and relevant training standards to commanders. All questions pertaining to the Marine Corps Ground T&R Program and Unit Training Management should be directed to: CG, TECOM (Ground Training Division C 469), 1019 Elliot Road, Quantico, VA 22134.

5. _Command_. This Manual is applicable to the Marine Corps Total Force.

6. _Certification_. Reviewed and approved this date.


R. C. FOX
By direction

DISTRIBUTION: PCN 10031979800

Copy to: 7000260 (2)
8145001 (1)

LOCATOR SHEET

Subj:   COMBAT CAMERA (COMCAM) TRAINING AND READINESS (T&R) MANUAL

Location:   _____
              (Indicate location(s) of copy(ies) of this Manual.)

RECORD OF CHANGES

Log completed change action as indicated.

| Change Number | Date of Change | Date Entered | Signature of Person Incorporated Change |
|---|---|---|---|
| | | | |
| | | | |
| | | | |
| | | | |
| | | | |
| | | | |
| | | | |
| | | | |
| | | | |
| | | | |

## TABLE OF CONTENTS

COMCAM T&R MANUAL

CHAPTER 1

OVERVIEW

CHAPTER 1

OVERVIEW

## 1000. INTRODUCTION

1. The T&R Program is the Corps' primary tool for planning, conducting and evaluating training and assessing training readiness. Subject matter experts (SMEs) from the operating forces developed core capability Mission Essential Task Lists (METLs) for ground communities derived from the Marine Corps Task List (MCTL). This T&R Manual is built around these METLs and other related Marine Corps Tasks (MCT). All events contained in the manual relate directly to these METLs and MCTs. This comprehensive T&R Program will help to ensure the Marine Corps continues to improve its combat readiness by training more efficiently and effectively. Ultimately, this will enhance the Marine Corps' ability to accomplish real-world missions.

2. The T&R Manual contains the individual and collective training requirements to prepare units to accomplish their combat mission. The T&R Manual is not intended to be an encyclopedia that contains every minute detail of how to accomplish training. Instead, it identifies the minimum standards that Marines must be able to perform in combat. The T&R Manual is a fundamental tool for commanders to build and maintain unit combat readiness. Using this tool, leaders can construct and execute an effective training plan that supports the unit's METL. More detailed information on the Marine Corps Ground T&R Program is found in reference (a).

3. The T&R Manual is designed for use by unit commanders to determine pre-deployment training requirements in preparation for training and for Formal Learning Centers and Training Detachments to create courses of instruction. This directive focuses on individual and collective tasks performed by operating forces (OPFOR) units and supervised by personnel in the performance of unit Mission Essential Tasks (METs).

## 1001. UNIT TRAINING

1. The training of Marines to perform as an integrated unit in combat lies at the heart of the T&R program. Unit and individual readiness are directly related. Individual training and the mastery of individual core skills serve as the building blocks for unit combat readiness. A Marine's ability to perform critical skills required in combat is essential. However, it is not necessary to have all individuals within a unit fully trained in order for that organization to accomplish its assigned tasks. Manpower shortfalls, temporary assignments, leave, or other factors outside the commander's control, often affect the ability to conduct individual training. During these periods, unit readiness is enhanced if emphasis is placed on the individual training of Marines on-hand. Subsequently, these Marines will be mission ready and capable of executing as part of a team when the full complement of personnel is available.

2.  Commanders will ensure that all tactical training is focused on their combat mission.  The T&R Manual is a tool to help develop the unit's training plan.  In most cases, unit training should focus on achieving unit proficiency in the core METL.  However, commanders will adjust their training focus to support METLs associated with a major OPLAN/CONPLAN or named operation as designated by their higher commander and reported accordingly in the Defense Readiness Reporting System (DRRS).  Tactical training will support the METL in use by the commander and be tailored to meet T&R standards.  Commanders at all levels are responsible for effective combat training.  The conduct of training in a professional manner consistent with Marine Corps standards cannot be over emphasized.

3.  Commanders will provide personnel the opportunity to attend formal and operational level courses of instruction as required by this manual. Attendance at all formal courses must enhance the warfighting capabilities of the unit as determined by the unit commander.

## 1002.  UNIT TRAINING MANAGEMENT

1.  Unit Training Management (UTM) is the application of the Systems Approach to Training (SAT) and the Marine Corps Training Principles.  This is accomplished in a manner that maximizes training results and focuses the training priorities of the unit in preparation for the conduct of its wartime mission.

2.  UTM techniques, described in references (b) and (e), provide commanders with the requisite tools and techniques to analyze, design, develop, implement, and evaluate the training of their unit.  The Marine Corps Training Principles, explained in reference (b), provide sound and proven direction and are flexible enough to accommodate the demands of local conditions.  These principles are not inclusive, nor do they guarantee success.  They are guides that commanders can use to manage unit-training programs.  The Marine Corps training principles are:

- Train as you fight
- Make commanders responsible for training
- Use standards-based training
- Use performance-oriented training
- Use mission-oriented training
- Train the MAGTF to fight as a combined arms team
- Train to sustain proficiency
- Train to challenge

3.  To maintain an efficient and effective training program, leaders at every level must understand and implement UTM.  Guidance for UTM and the process for establishing effective programs are contained in references (b), (e) and (f).

## 1003.  SUSTAINMENT AND EVALUATION OF TRAINING

1.  The evaluation of training is necessary to properly prepare Marines for combat.  Evaluations are either formal or informal, and performed by members

of the unit (internal evaluation) or from an external command (external evaluation).

2. Marines are expected to maintain proficiency in the training events for their MOS at the appropriate grade or billet to which assigned. Leaders are responsible for recording the training achievements of their Marines. Whether it involves individual or collective training events, they must ensure proficiency is sustained by requiring retraining of each event at or before expiration of the designated sustainment interval. Performance of the training event, however, is not sufficient to ensure combat readiness. Leaders at all levels must evaluate the performance of their Marines and the unit as they complete training events, and only record successful accomplishment of training based upon the evaluation. The goal of evaluation is to ensure that correct methods are employed to achieve the desired standard, or the Marines understand how they need to improve in order to attain the standard. Leaders must determine whether credit for completing a training event is recorded if the standard was not achieved. While successful accomplishment is desired, debriefing of errors can result in successful learning that will allow ethical recording of training event completion. Evaluation is a continuous process that is integral to training management and is conducted by leaders at every level and during all phases of planning and the conduct of training. To ensure training is efficient and effective, evaluation is an integral part of the training plan. Ultimately, leaders remain responsible for determining if the training was effective.

3. The purpose of formal and informal evaluation is to provide commanders with a process to determine a unit's/Marine's proficiency in the tasks that must be performed in combat. Informal evaluations are conducted during every training evolution. Formal evaluations are often scenario-based, focused on the unit's METs, based on collective training standards, and usually conducted during higher-level collective events. References (a) and (f) provide further guidance on the conduct of informal and formal evaluations using the Marine Corps Ground T&R Program.

**1004. ORGANIZATION.** The Combat Camera T&R Manual is comprised of 8 chapters. Chapter 2 lists the Combat Camera Core METs. Chapter 3 contains collective events for Combat Camera Teams (3000-level) and Sections (4000-level). Chapters 4 through 8 contain individual events for the entire combat camera occupational field.

**1005. T&R EVENT CODING**

1. T&R events are coded for ease of reference. Each event has a 4-4-4-digit identifier. The first four digits are referred to as a "community" and represent the MOS. The second four digits represent the functional or duty area (PLAN, OPER, PROT, etc.). The last four digits represent the level, duty area and sequence of the event.

2. The T&R levels are illustrated in Figure 1. An example of the T&R coding used in this manual is shown in Figure 2.

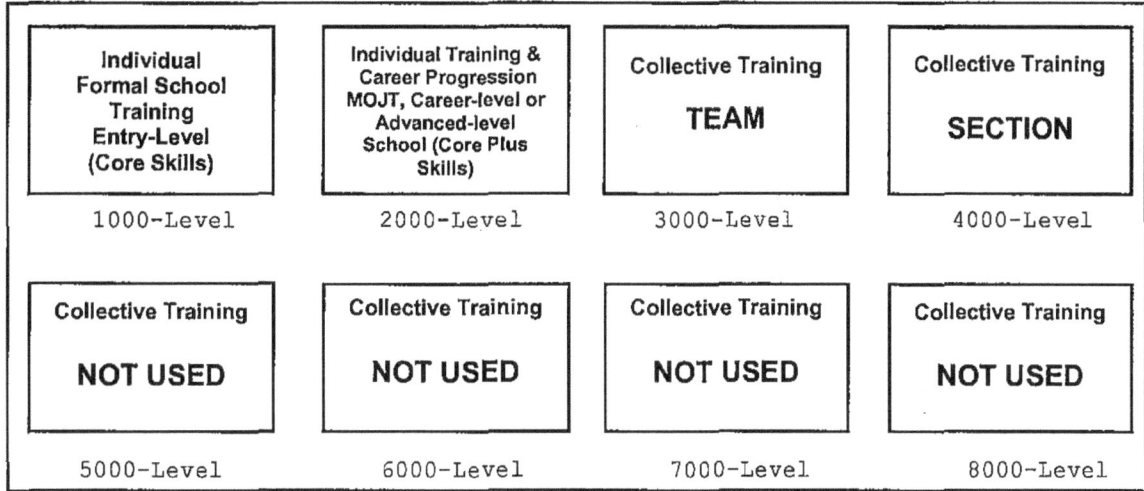

Figure 1:  T&R Event Levels

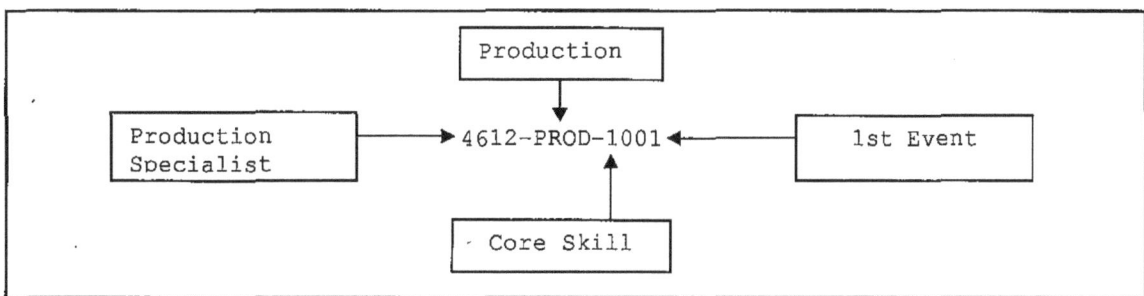

Figure 2:  T&R Event Coding

## 1006.  EVALUATION-CODED (E-CODED) EVENTS

1.  T&R Manuals can contain numerous unit events, some for the whole unit and others for integral parts that serve as building blocks for training.  To simplify training management and readiness assessment, only collective events that are critical components of a Mission Essential Task (MET), or key indicators of a unit's readiness, are used to generate CRP for a MET.  These critical or key events are designated in the T&R Manual as Evaluation-Coded (E-Coded) events because they directly support a MET on the METL.  Formal evaluation of unit performance in these events is recommended because of their value in assessing combat readiness.  Only E-Coded events are used to calculate CRP for each MET.

2.  The use of a METL-based training program allows the commander discretion in training.  This makes the T&R Manual a training tool rather than a prescriptive checklist.

**1007. COMBAT READINESS PERCENTAGE**

1. The Marine Corps Ground T&R Program includes processes to assess readiness of units and individual Marines. Every unit in the Marine Corps maintains a basic level of readiness based on the training and experience of the Marines in the unit. Even units that never trained together are capable of accomplishing some portion of their missions. Combat readiness assessment does not associate a quantitative value for this baseline of readiness, but uses a "Combat Readiness Percentage", as a method to provide a concise descriptor of the recent training accomplishments of units and Marines.

2. Combat Readiness Percentage (CRP) is the percentage of required training events that a unit or Marine accomplishes within specified sustainment intervals.

3. Unit combat readiness is assessed as a percentage of the successfully completed and current (within sustainment interval) key training events called "Evaluation-Coded" (E-Coded) Events. E-Coded Events and unit CRP calculation are described in follow-on paragraphs. CRP achieved through the completion of E-Coded Events is directly relevant to readiness assessment in DRRS.

4. Individual combat readiness is assessed as the percentage of required individual events in which a Marine is current. This translates as the percentage of training events for his/her MOS and grade that the Marine successfully completes within the directed sustainment interval. Individual skills are developed through a combination of 1000-level training (entry-level formal school courses), individual on-the-job training in 2000-level events, and follow-on formal school training. Skill proficiency is maintained by retraining in each event per the specified sustainment interval.

**1008. CRP CALCULATION**

1. Collective training begins at the 3000-level (team, crew or equivalent). Unit training plans are designed to accomplish the events that support the unit METL while simultaneously sustaining proficiency in individual core skills. E-Coded collective events are the only events that contribute to unit CRP. This is done to assist commanders in prioritizing the training toward the METL, taking into account resource, time, and personnel constraints.

2. Unit CRP increases after the completion of E-Coded events. The number of E-Coded events for the MET determines the value of each E-Coded event. For example, if there are 4 E-Coded events for a MET, each is worth 25% of MET CRP. MET CRP is calculated by adding the percentage of each completed and current (within sustainment interval) E-Coded training event. The percentage for each MET is calculated the same way and all are added together and divided by the number of METS to determine unit CRP. For ease of calculation, we will say that each MET has four E-Coded events, each contributing 25% towards the completion of the MET. If the unit has completed and is current on three of the four E-Coded events for a given MET, then they have completed 75% of the MET. The CRP for each MET is added

together and divided by the number of METS to get unit CRP; unit CRP is the average of MET CRP.
For Example:

```
MET 1:  75% complete  (3 of 4 E-Coded events trained)
MET 2:  100% complete (6 of 6 E-Coded events trained)
MET 3:  25% complete  (1 of 4 E-Coded events trained)
MET 4:  50% complete  (2 of 4 E-Coded events trained)
MET 5:  75% complete  (3 of 4 E-Coded events trained)
```

To get unit CRP, simply add the CRP for each MET and divide by the number of METS:

MET CRP:  75 + 100 + 25 + 50 + 75 = 325

Unit CRP:  325 (total MET CRP)/5 (total number of METS) = 65%


## 1009. T&R EVENT COMPOSITION

1.  This section explains each of the components of a T&R event.  Some of the components listed below are not included in the events within this T&R manual.

    a.  Event Code (see Sect 1005).  The event code is an up to 4-4-4 character set.  For individual training events, the first four characters indicate the occupational function.  The second up to four characters indicate functional area (PLAN = 1, OPER = 5, PROT = 8, etc.).  The third four characters are simply a numerical designator / sequence for the event.

    b.  Event Title.  The event title is the name of the event (behavior).

    c.  E-Coded.  This is a "yes/no" category to indicate whether the event is E-Coded.  If yes, the event contributes toward the CRP of the associated MET.  The value of each E-Coded event is based on number of E-Coded events for that MET.  Refer to paragraph 1007 for detailed explanation of E-Coded events.

    d.  Supported MET(s).  List all METs that are supported by the training event.

    e.  Sustainment Interval.  This is the period, expressed in number of months, between evaluation or retraining requirements.  Skills and capabilities acquired through the accomplishment of training events are refreshed at pre-determined intervals.  It is essential that these intervals are adhered to in order to ensure Marines maintain proficiency.

    f.  Billet.  Individual training events may contain a list of billets within the community that are responsible for performing that event.  This ensures that the billets expected tasks are clearly articulated and a Marine's readiness to perform in that billet is measured.

    g.  Grade.  Each individual training event will list the rank(s) at which Marines are required to learn and sustain the training event.

h.  <u>Initial Training Setting</u>.  Specifies the location for initial instruction of the training event in one of three categories (formal school, managed on-the-job training, distance learning).  Regardless of the specified Initial Training Setting, any T&R event may be introduced and evaluated during managed on-the-job training.

(1) "Formal" - When the Initial Training Setting of an event is identified as "FORMAL" (formal school), the appropriate formal school or training detachment is required to provide initial training in the event. Conversely, formal schools and training detachments are not authorized to provide training in events designated as Initial Training Setting "MOJT" or "DL."  Since the duration of formal school training must be constrained to optimize Operating Forces' manning, this element provides the mechanism for Operating Forces' prioritization of training requirements.  For formal schools and training detachments, this element defines the requirements for content of courses.

(2) "DL" - Identifies the training event as a candidate for initial training via a Distance Learning product (correspondence course or MarineNet course).

(3) "MOJT" - Events specified for Managed On-the-Job Training are to be introduced to Marines as part of training within a unit by supervisory personnel.

i.  <u>Event Description</u>.  Provide a description of the event purpose, objectives, goals, and requirements.  It is a general description of an action requiring learned skills and knowledge (e.g. Camouflage the M1A1 Tank).

j.  <u>Condition</u>.  Describe the condition(s), under which tasks are performed.  Conditions are based on a "real world" operational environment. They indicate what is provided (equipment, materials, manuals, aids, etc.), environmental constraints, conditions under which the task is performed, and any specific cues or indicators to which the performer must respond.  When resources or safety requirements limit the conditions, this is stated.

k.  <u>Standard</u>.  The standard indicates the basis for judging effectiveness of the performance.  It consists of a carefully worded statement that identifies the proficiency level expected when the task is performed.  The standard provides the minimum acceptable performance parameters and is strictly adhered to.  The standard for collective events is general, describing the desired end-state or purpose of the event.  While the standard for individual events specifically describe to what proficiency level in terms of accuracy, speed, sequencing, quality of performance, adherence to procedural guidelines, etc., the event is accomplished.

l.  <u>Event Components</u>.  Describe the actions composing the event and help the user determine what must be accomplished to properly plan for the event.

m.  <u>Prerequisite Events</u>.  Prerequisites are academic training or other T&R events that must be completed prior to attempting the task.  They are lower-level events or tasks that give the individual/unit the skills required to accomplish the event.  They can also be planning steps, administrative requirements, or specific parameters that build toward mission accomplishment.

n. <u>Chained Events</u>. Collective T&R events are supported by lower-level collective and individual T&R events. This enables unit leaders to effectively identify subordinate T&R events that ultimately support specific mission essential tasks. When the accomplishment of any upper-level events, by their nature, result in the performance of certain subordinate and related events, the events are "chained." The completion of chained events will update sustainment interval credit (and CRP for E-Coded events) for the related subordinate level events.

o. <u>Related Events</u>. Provide a list of all Individual Training Standards that support the event.

p. <u>References</u>. The training references are utilized to determine task performance steps, grading criteria, and ensure standardization of training procedures. They assist the trainee in satisfying the performance standards, or the trainer in evaluating the effectiveness of task completion. References are also important to the development of detailed training plans.

q. <u>Distance Learning Products</u> (IMI, CBT, MCI, etc.). Include this component when the event can be taught via one of these media methods vice attending a formal course of instruction or receiving MOJT.

r. <u>Support Requirements</u>. This is a list of the external and internal support the unit and Marines will need to complete the event. The list includes, but is not limited to:

- Range(s)/Training Area
- Ordnance
- Equipment
- Materials
- Other Units/Personnel
- Other Support Requirements

s. <u>Miscellaneous</u>. Provide any additional information that assists in the planning and execution of the event. Miscellaneous information may include, but is not limited to:

- Admin Instructions
- Special Personnel Certifications
- Equipment Operating Hours
- Road Miles

## 1010. CBRN TRAINING

1. All personnel assigned to the operating force must be trained in chemical, biological, radiological, and nuclear defense (CBRN), in order to survive and continue their mission in this environment. Individual proficiency standards are defined as survival and basic operating standards. Survival standards are those that the individual must master in order to survive CBRN attacks. Basic operating standards are those that the

individual, and collectively the unit, must perform to continue operations in a CBRN environment.

2. In order to develop and maintain the ability to operate in a CBRN environment, CBRN training is an integral part of the training plan and events in this T&R Manual. Units should train under CBRN conditions whenever possible. Per reference (c), all units must be capable of accomplishing their assigned mission in a contaminated environment.

## 1011. NIGHT TRAINING

1. While it is understood that all personnel and units of the operating force are capable of performing their assigned mission in "every climate and place," current doctrine emphasizes the requirement to perform assigned missions at night and during periods of limited visibility. Basic skills are significantly more difficult when visibility is limited.

2. To ensure units are capable of accomplishing their mission they must train under the conditions of limited visibility. Units should strive to conduct all events in this T&R Manual during both day and night/limited visibility conditions. When there is limited training time available, night training should take precedence over daylight training, contingent on the availability of equipment and personnel.

## 1012. OPERATIONAL RISK MANAGEMENT (ORM)

1. ORM is a process that enables commanders to plan for and minimize risk while still accomplishing the mission. It is a decision making tool used by Marines at all levels to increase operational effectiveness by anticipating hazards and reducing the potential for loss, thereby increasing the probability of a successful mission. ORM minimizes risks to acceptable levels, commensurate with mission accomplishment.

2. Commanders, leaders, maintainers, planners, and schedulers will integrate risk assessment in the decision-making process and implement hazard controls to reduce risk to acceptable levels. Applying the ORM process will reduce mishaps, lower costs, and provide for more efficient use of resources. ORM assists the commander in conserving lives and resources and avoiding unnecessary risk, making an informed decision to implement a Course Of Action (COA), identifying feasible and effective control measures where specific measures do not exist, and providing reasonable alternatives for mission accomplishment. Most importantly, ORM assists the commander in determining the balance between training realism and unnecessary risks in training, the impact of training operations on the environment, and the adjustment of training plans to fit the level of proficiency and experience of Sailors/Marines and leaders. Further guidance for ORM is found in references (b) and (d).

## 1013. APPLICATION OF SIMULATION

1. Simulations/Simulators and other training devices shall be used when they are capable of effectively and economically supplementing training on the

identified training task. Particular emphasis shall be placed on simulators that provide training that might be limited by safety considerations or constraints on training space, time, or other resources. When deciding on simulation issues, the primary consideration shall be improving the quality of training and consequently the state of readiness. Potential savings in operating and support costs normally shall be an important secondary consideration.

2. Each training event contains information relating to the applicability of simulation. If simulator training applies to the event, then the applicable simulator(s) is/are listed in the "Simulation" section and the CRP for simulation training is given. This simulation training can either be used in place of live training, at the reduced CRP indicated; or can be used as a precursor training for the live event, i.e., weapons simulators, convoy trainers, observed fire trainers, etc. It is recommended that tasks be performed by simulation prior to being performed in a live-fire environment. However, in the case where simulation is used as a precursor for the live event, then the unit will receive credit for the live event CRP only. If a tactical situation develops that precludes performing the live event, the unit would then receive credit for the simulation CRP.

## 1014. MARINE CORPS GROUND T&R PROGRAM

1. The Marine Corps Ground T&R Program continues to evolve. The vision for Ground T&R Program is to publish a T&R Manual for every readiness-reporting unit so that core capability METs are clearly defined with supporting collective training standards, and to publish community-based T&R Manuals for all occupational fields whose personnel augment other units to increase their combat and/or logistic capabilities. The vision for this program includes plans to provide a Marine Corps training management information system that enables tracking of unit and individual training accomplishments by unit commanders and small unit leaders, automatically computing CRP for both units and individual Marines based upon MOS and rank (or billet). Linkage of T&R Events to the Marine Corps Task List (MCTL), through the core capability METs, has enabled objective assessment of training readiness in the DRRS.

2. DRRS measures and reports on the readiness of military forces and the supporting infrastructure to meet missions and goals assigned by the Secretary of Defense. With unit CRP based on the unit's training toward its METs, the CRP will provide a more accurate picture of a unit's readiness. This will give fidelity to future funding requests and factor into the allocation of resources. Additionally, the Ground T&R Program will help to ensure training remains focused on mission accomplishment and that training readiness reporting is tied to units' METLs.

COMCAM T&R MANUAL

CHAPTER 2

MISSION ESSENTIAL TASKS MATRIX

COMCAM T&R MANUAL

CHAPTER 2

MISSION ESSENTIAL TASKS MATRIX

**2000. COMCAM COMMUNITY CORE MISSION ESSENTIAL TASK LIST (METL).** The COMCAM Community METL Table lists the Standardized Core Mission Essential Tasks (MET), derived from the Marine Corps Task List (MCTL), for the COMCAM Community. This METL is used for readiness reporting in the Defense Readiness Reporting System (DRRS).

| MARINE CORPS TASK LIST | COMCAM COMMUNITY CORE METL |
|---|---|
| MCT 3.1.6.1.4 | Provide For Combat Camera and Tactical Printing In Theater |
| MCT 3.1.6.1.5 | Provide Combat Camera Support Services |

**2001. COMCAM COMMUNITY MISSION ESSENTIAL TASKS (MET) MATRIX**

**MET#/MISSION ESSENTIAL TASK**

| MET 1. PROVIDE FOR COMBAT CAMERA AND TACTICAL PRINTING IN THEATER | |
|---|---|
| CCAM-MNGT-4001 | Employ Tactical Imagery Production System |
| CCAM-MNGT-3001 | Conduct Combat Camera Actions in Support of Operational/ Training Requirements |
| **MET 2. PROVIDE COMBAT CAMERA SUPPORT SERVICES** | |
| CCAM-MNGT-4001 | Employ Tactical Imagery Production System |
| CCAM-MNGT-3001 | Conduct Combat Camera Actions in Support of Operational/ Training Requirements |

COMCAM T&R MANUAL

CHAPTER 3

COLLECTIVE EVENTS

CHAPTER 3

COLLECTIVE EVENTS

3000.  **PURPOSE**.  Chapter 3 contains collective training events for the Combat Camera Community.

3001.  **EVENT CODING**.  Events in this T&R Manual are depicted with an up to 12-character, 3-field alphanumeric system, i.e. XXXX-XXXX-XXXX.  This chapter utilizes the following methodology:

   a.  Field one.  This field represents the community.  This chapter contains the following community codes:

| Code | Description |
|------|-------------|
| CCAM | Combat Camera |

   b.  Field two.  This field represents the functional/duty area.  This chapter contains the following functional/duty areas:

| Code | Description |
|------|-------------|
| MNGT | Management |

   c.  Field three.  This field provides the level at which the event is accomplished and numerical sequencing of events.  This chapter contains the following event levels:

| Code | Description |
|------|-------------|
| 4000 | Section Level |
| 3000 | Team Level |

3002.  INDEX OF COLLECTIVE EVENTS

| Event Code | E-Coded | Event | Page |
|---|---|---|---|
| 4000-LEVEL | | | |
| CCAM-MNGT-4001 | Y | Employ Tactical Imagery Production System | 3-4 |
| 3000-LEVEL | | | |
| CCAM-MNGT-3001 | Y | Conduct Combat Camera Actions in Support of Operational/Training Requirements | 3-5 |

3003. 4000-LEVEL EVENTS

**CCAM-MNGT-4001:** Employ Tactical Imagery Production System

**SUPPORTED MET(S):** 1, 2

**EVALUATION-CODED:** YES          **SUSTAINMENT INTERVAL:** 12 months

**DESCRIPTION:** Marines will setup and employ the Tactical Imagery Production System (TIPS). A minimum of 9 and no more than 12 COMCAM personnel are required to employ the TIPS.

**CONDITION:** With the aid of references, given a requirement, a Tactical Imagery Production System, 9 personnel, and logistical support.

**STANDARD:** In event component sequence, to produce COMCAM products, in a timeline established by the commander, and in accordance with the references.

**EVENT COMPONENTS:**
1. Produce COMCAM products.
2. Execute CLS agreement; as required.
3. Disassemble tactical imagery production system.
4. Prepare for redeployment; as required.
5. Initiate all SL3 components.
6. Troubleshoot all SL3 components.
7. Operate all SL3 components.
8. Setup tactical imagery production system.
9. Implement logistics support plan.

**REFERENCES:**
1. MCO 3104.1_ Marine Corps Combat Camera Program
2. MCWP 3-33.7 Combat Camera in the MAGTF
3. SOP Standard Operating Procedures (SOP)
4. TIPS Manual Tactical Imagery Production System (TIPS) Training Manual
5. TM 10-5411-200-14 Shelter, Tactical, Expandable, Two-Sided (Tactical Imagery Production System)
6. TM 11084A-OI Environmental Control Unit

**SUPPORT REQUIREMENTS:**

**UNITS/PERSONNEL:** Support personnel required; 1341 Generator Mechanic, 1161 Environmental Control Unit Mechanic, 3531 Motor Vehicle Operator, 3521 Organizational Auto Mechanic, 4068 Data Network Technician, 0651 Data Network Specialist, 0656 Tactical Network Specialist.

**MISCELLANEOUS:**

**ADMINISTRATIVE INSTRUCTIONS:** The Tactical Imagery Production System (TIPS) has organic photographic, video, multimedia, reproduction and printing capabilities. The system is supported by both Continued Logistics Support (CLS) for Commercial off the Shelf (COTS) equipment (computers, printers, dub racks, etc) and though local organic engineering support for the Government Off the Shelf (GOTS) equipment (generators, environmental control units, etc). The TIPS has the capability to attach to local command communication assets.

**3004. 3000-LEVEL EVENTS**

**CCAM-MNGT-3001**: Conduct Combat Camera Actions in support of Operational/ Training requirements

**SUPPORTED MET(S)**: 1, 2

**EVALUATION-CODED**: YES          **SUSTAINMENT INTERVAL**: 12 months

**DESCRIPTION**: Marines will design and develop multimedia products in support of operational and training requirements.

**CONDITION**: With the aid of reference, given a TIPS or production workstation, associated software/materials, production equipment, and a requirement.

**STANDARD**: Fulfilling mission requirements in accordance with the commander's intent.

**EVENT COMPONENTS**:
1. Receive requirement.
2. Identify environment.
3. Acquire imagery.
4. Create illustrations.
5. Mass reproduce products.
6. Assign teams.
7. Create products of multiple mediums.
8. Perform quality control.
9. Validate product meets requirement.
10. Archive finished product.
11. Transmit imagery/products.
12. Accession products.

**REFERENCES**:
1. Current Standard Operating Procedures (SOP) from Higher Headquarters

**MISCELLANEOUS**:

   **ADMINISTRATIVE INSTRUCTIONS**: Includes all operations conducted by the MAGTF (specifically Information Operations (IO) and Missions In Support Of Operations (MISO), training commands and support establishments.

---

COMCAM T&R MANUAL

CHAPTER 4

MOS 4602 INDIVIDUAL EVENTS

CHAPTER 4

MOS 4602 INDIVIDUAL EVENTS

**4000. PURPOSE.** This chapter details the individual events that pertain to MOS 4602, Combat Camera Officer. These events are linked to a service-level Mission Essential Tasks (MET). This link tailors individual training for the selected MET. Each individual event provides an event title, along with the conditions events will be performed under, and the standard to which the event must be performed to be successful.

**4001. EVENT CODING.** Events in this T&R Manual are depicted with an up to 12-character, 3-field alphanumeric system, i.e. XXXX-XXXX-XXXX. This chapter utilizes the following methodology:

    a. Field one. This field represents the community. This chapter contains the following community codes:

| Code | Description |
|------|-------------|
| 4602 | Combat Camera Officer |

    b. Field two. This field represents the functional/duty area. This chapter contains the following functional/duty areas:

| Code | Description |
|------|-------------|
| MNGT | Management |
| PLAN | Planning |

    c. Field three. This field provides the level at which the event is accomplished and numerical sequencing of events. This chapter contains the following event levels:

| Code | Description |
|------|-------------|
| 2000 | Core Plus Skills |

4002.  INDEX OF INDIVIDUAL EVENTS

| Event Code | Event | Page |
|---|---|---|
| | MANAGEMENT | |
| 4602-MNGT-2001 | Conduct a COMCAM capabilities brief | 4-4 |
| 4602-MNGT-2002 | Develop Appendix 9, Annex C to an Operations Order | 4-4 |
| 4602-MNGT-2003 | Develop COMCAM Standard Operating Procedures (SOP) | 4-5 |
| 4602-MNGT-2004 | Develop local COMCAM Order (3104.1) | 4-6 |
| 4602-MNGT-2005 | Direct the employment of the Tactical Imagery Production System (TIPS) | 4-6 |
| 4602-MNGT-2006 | Implement the Safety and Hazardous Material Plan | 4-7 |
| 4602-MNGT-2007 | Prepare Reports | 4-8 |
| 4602-MNGT-2008 | Develop an official naval correspondence | 4-8 |
| 4602-MNGT-2009 | Manage COMCAM budget | 4-9 |
| 4602-MNGT-2010 | Supervise the handling of classified material | 4-10 |
| 4602-MNGT-2011 | Submit lessons learned | 4-11 |
| 4602-MNGT-2012 | Manage COMCAM assets | 4-11 |
| 4602-MNGT-2013 | Establish imagery movement plan | 4-12 |
| 4602-MNGT-2014 | Manage a Production | 4-13 |
| | PLANNING | |
| 4602-PLAN-2015 | Direct embarkation of COMCAM equipment | 4-13 |
| 4602-PLAN-2016 | Develop the print management program | 4-14 |

**4003.  2000-LEVEL EVENTS**

**4602-MNGT-2001:**  Conduct a COMCAM capabilities brief

**EVALUATION-CODED:**  NO       **SUSTAINMENT INTERVAL:**  12 months

**DESCRIPTION:**  Marine will conduct a COMCAM Capabilities Brief in order to educate target audience on the capabilities and limitations of Marine Combat Camera which will assist in the proper employment of COMCAM assets.

**MOS PERFORMING:**  4602

**GRADES:**  WO-1, CWO-2, CWO-3, CWO-4, CWO-5, CAPT, MAJ, LTCOL

**INITIAL TRAINING SETTING:**  MOJT

**CONDITION:**  With the aid of references, given a requirement, a production work station, briefing format, briefing materials, and a target audience.

**STANDARD:**  Ensuring COMCAM capabilities and limitations are fully explained, within the time allotted and in accordance with the Marine Corps Combat Camera Program.

**PERFORMANCE STEPS:**
1.  Review the references.
2.  Prepare the brief.
3.  Prepare handouts; as required.
4.  Rehearse the brief.
5.  Conduct the brief.
6.  Answer questions.

**REFERENCES:**
1.  MCO 3104.1_ Marine Corps Combat Camera Program
2.  MCWP 3-33.7 Combat Camera in the MAGTF
3.  Local Standing Operating Procedures (SOP)
4.  Operations order (as applicable)

---

**4602-MNGT-2002:**  Develop Appendix 9, Annex C to an Operations Order

**EVALUATION-CODED:**  NO       **SUSTAINMENT INTERVAL:**  12 months

**DESCRIPTION:**  Marine will develop the Appendix 9, Annex C to an OPORD for submission to the Operations Officer.

**MOS PERFORMING:**  4602

**GRADES:**  WO-1, CWO-2, CWO-3, CWO-4, CWO-5, CAPT, MAJ, LTCOL

**INITIAL TRAINING SETTING:**  FORMAL

**CONDITION:**  With the aid of references, given an operations plan, template, and computer workstation.

STANDARD: Supporting the commander's intent and mission in a designated timeline.

PERFORMANCE STEPS:
1. Review operations plan.
2. Identify COMCAM assets.
3. Identify COMCAM functions.
4. Identify COMCAM responsibilities.
5. Identify COMCAM command structure.
6. Identify COMCAM reporting procedures.
7. Identify COMCAM planned employment.
8. Identify COMCAM coordinating instructions.
9. Identify COMCAM related operational parameters.
10. Finalize Appendix 9, Annex C.
11. Submit Appendix 9, Annex C to Operations Officer.

REFERENCES:
1. JCS PUB 1-02 DoD Dictionary of Military and Associated Terms
2. MCWP 3-33.7 Combat Camera in the MAGTF
3. MCWP 5-1 Marine Corps Planning Process (MCPP)
4. NAVMC/MCO 3000.18 Marine Corps Planner's Manual

---

**4602-MNGT-2003:** Develop COMCAM Standard Operating Procedures (SOP)

EVALUATION-CODED: NO          SUSTAINMENT INTERVAL: 12 months

DESCRIPTION: Marine will establish policy, standard operating procedures and desktop procedures that are compliant with appropriate MCO's, command directives, public laws, and follows the commander's intent.

MOS PERFORMING: 4602

GRADES: WO-1, CWO-2, CWO-3, CWO-4, CWO-5, CAPT, MAJ, LTCOL

INITIAL TRAINING SETTING: FORMAL

CONDITION: With the aid of references, given command directives and orders.

STANDARD: Within 90 days of assignment, and in accordance with Marine Corps Combat Camera Program.

PERFORMANCE STEPS:
1. Review current SOP.
2. Review local directives and policies.
3. Solicit input from COMCAM staff.
4. Draft SOP.
5. Submit to higher for review.
6. Publish SOP.
7. Review final SOP with COMCAM staff for compliance.
8. Update as required.

REFERENCES:
1. Local CC Program Local COMCAM 3104.1_

2.  MCO 3104.1_ Marine Corps Combat Camera Program
3.  MCWP 3-33.7 Combat Camera in the MAGTF
4.  Local Standing Operating Procedures (SOP)

---

**4602-MNGT-2004:** Develop local COMCAM Order (3104.1)

**EVALUATION-CODED:** NO          **SUSTAINMENT INTERVAL:** 12 months

**DESCRIPTION:** Marine will develop a local COMCAM Order which outlines COMCAM actions and services derived from MCO 3104.1 and contain local SOP.

**MOS PERFORMING:** 4602

**GRADES:** WO-1, CWO-2, CWO-3, CWO-4, CWO-5, CAPT, MAJ, LTCOL

**INITIAL TRAINING SETTING:** MOJT

**CONDITION:** With the aid of references, given command directives and orders and a workstation.

**STANDARD:** Within 90 days of assignment, that meets commander's intent.

**PERFORMANCE STEPS:**
1.  Review references.
2.  Review local directives and policies.
3.  Draft order.
4.  Submit to higher for review.
5.  Make modifications; as required.
6.  Submit for publication.
7.  Review published order with COMCAM staff.
8.  Update as required.

**REFERENCES:**
1.  Local CC Program Local COMCAM 3104.1_
2.  MCO 3104.1_ Marine Corps Combat Camera Program
3.  MCWP 3-33.7 Combat Camera in the MAGTF

---

**4602-MNGT-2005:** Direct the employment of the Tactical Imagery Production System (TIPS)

**EVALUATION-CODED:** NO          **SUSTAINMENT INTERVAL:** 12 months

**DESCRIPTION:** Marine will direct the employment and operation of the Tactical Imagery Production System (TIPS).

**MOS PERFORMING:** 4602

**GRADES:** WO-1, CWO-2, CWO-3, CWO-4, CWO-5, CAPT, MAJ, LTCOL

**INITIAL TRAINING SETTING:** FORMAL

**CONDITION:** With the aid of references, given a mission, TIPS, COMCAM personnel, logistical support, and a location to set up.

**STANDARD:** In performance step sequence, to support operational requirements, in a timeline established by the commander.

**PERFORMANCE STEPS:**
1. Ensure TIPS employment plan is included in operations.
2. Conduct site survey.
3. Arrange for logistical support with S/G-4.
4. Direct TIPS assembly.
5. Ensure safety guidelines are followed.
6. Ensure systems/operations checks are completed.
7. Direct TIPS operations.
8. Direct TIPS disassembly.
9. Plan for redeployment; as required.

**REFERENCES:**
1. MCO 3104.1_ Marine Corps Combat Camera Program
2. MCWP 3-33.7 Combat Camera in the MAGTF
3. Operator's Manual Operator's Manual
4. SL-3-4120 Family of Environmental Control Units
5. SL-3-6115 Generator Set, Diesel Engine Driven, Skid Mounted
6. SOP Standard Operating Procedures (SOP)
7. TM 10-5411-200-14 Shelter, Tactical, Expandable, Two-Sided (Tactical Imagery Production System)

**SUPPORT REQUIREMENTS:**

**UNITS/PERSONNEL:** 1341 Generator Mechanic, 1161 Environmental Control Unit Mechanic, 3531 Motor Vehicle Operator, 3521 Organizational Auto Mechanic, 4068 Data Network Technician, 0651 Data Network Specialist, 0656 Tactical Network Specialist and 0411 Maintenance Management Specialist.

---

**4602-MNGT-2006:** Implement the Safety and Hazardous Material Plan

**EVALUATION-CODED:** NO          **SUSTAINMENT INTERVAL:** 12 months

**DESCRIPTION:** Marine will implement (if not already implemented), manage, and maintain unit safety and hazardous material plan

**MOS PERFORMING:** 4602

**GRADES:** WO-1, CWO-2, CWO-3, CWO-4, CWO-5, CAPT, MAJ, LTCOL

**INITIAL TRAINING SETTING:** MOJT

**CONDITION:** With the aid of references, given local command policy and directives.

**STANDARD:** Ensuring compliance with safety and hazardous material regulations.

**PERFORMANCE STEPS:**
1. Identify Combat Camera Unit hazardous materials.
2. Coordinate safety and hazmat training.
3. Establish safety and hazmat procedures.
4. Assign a Safety NCO; as required.
5. Assign a HAZMAT NCO; as required.
6. Supervise safety and hazmat plan execution.

**REFERENCES:**
1. DoD 6050.5 Hazardous Material Information System User's Guide
2. MCO 5100.29_ Marine Corps Safety Program
3. MCO 5100.30B Marine Corps Off-Duty and Recreation Safety Program (July 08)
4. MCO P4400.150_ Consumer Level Supply Policy Manual
5. MCO P5090.2A Environmental Compliance and Protection Manual (Jul 98)
6. Local Standing Operating Procedures (SOP)

---

**4602-MNGT-2007:** Prepare Reports

**EVALUATION-CODED:** NO          **SUSTAINMENT INTERVAL:** 12 months

**DESCRIPTION:** Marine will compile data from COMCAM sections for statistical and budgetary review and submission to higher.

**MOS PERFORMING:** 4602

**GRADES:** WO-1, CWO-2, CWO-3, CWO-4, CWO-5, CAPT, MAJ, LTCOL

**INITIAL TRAINING SETTING:** FORMAL

**CONDITION:** With the aid of references, given access to the Combat Camera Management job order database, Common Access Card (CAC) enabled production workstation, and associated software.

**STANDARD:** Within a timeline established by the commander.

**PERFORMANCE STEPS:**
1. Access job order database.
2. Select records.
3. Generate report.
4. Submit report; as required.

**REFERENCES:**
1. JODUM Job Order Database Users Manual
2. MCO 3104.1_ Marine Corps Combat Camera Program
3. Local Standing Operating Procedures (SOP)

---

**4602-MNGT-2008:** Develop an official naval correspondence

**EVALUATION-CODED:** NO          **SUSTAINMENT INTERVAL:** 12 months

DESCRIPTION: Marine will draft a naval message to communicate official correspondence.

MOS PERFORMING: 4602

GRADES: WO-1, CWO-2, CWO-3, CWO-4, CWO-5, CAPT, MAJ, LTCOL

INITIAL TRAINING SETTING: FORMAL

CONDITION: With the aid of references, given the requirement to communicate official correspondence.

STANDARD: In performance step sequence, to meet the requirement, in accordance with SECNAVINST 5216.5.

PERFORMANCE STEPS:
1. Review the requirement.
2. Review the references.
3. Draft naval correspondence.
4. Submit naval correspondence for review.
5. Make corrections; as required.
6. Submit for distribution.
7. Confirm publication.

REFERENCES:
1. SECNAVINST 5216.5 Naval Correspondence Manual
2. USMTF Manual

---

4602-MNGT-2009: Manage COMCAM Budget

EVALUATION-CODED: NO          SUSTAINMENT INTERVAL: 12 months

DESCRIPTION: Marine will develop and execute COMCAM budget.

MOS PERFORMING: 4602

GRADES: WO-1, CWO-2, CWO-3, CWO-4, CWO-5, CAPT, MAJ, LTCOL

INITIAL TRAINING SETTING: FORMAL

CONDITION: Given historical data, existing contracts, CMR, list of existing deficiencies, life cycle management and operations & maintenance plans.

STANDARD: Ensuring that a budget plan is submitted that identifies all COMCAM requirements, and is executed in compliance with the Field Budget Guidance manual.

PERFORMANCE STEPS:
1. Review historical data.
2. Review life cycle management plan.
3. Review CMR.
4. Review existing deficiencies.
5. Draft budget plan.

6. Submit draft budget plan.
7. Review approved budget.
8. Identify fiscal deficiencies.
9. Submit unfunded deficiency request; as required.
10. Execute approved budget.
11. Maintain budget records.

**REFERENCES:**
1. MCO 3104.1_ Marine Corps Combat Camera Program
2. MCO P4400.150_ Consumer Level Supply Policy Manual
3. MCO P7100.8_ Field Budget Guidance Manual
4. Operator's Manual Operator's Manual
5. TM 4700-15/1_ Ground Equipment Record Procedures
6. Local Standing Operating Procedures (SOP)

---

**4602-MNGT-2010:** Supervise the handling of classified material

**EVALUATION-CODED:** NO          **SUSTAINMENT INTERVAL:** 12 months

**MOS PERFORMING:** 4602

**GRADES:** WO-1, CWO-2, CWO-3, CWO-4, CWO-5, CAPT, MAJ, LTCOL

**INITIAL TRAINING SETTING:** MOJT

**CONDITION:** With the aid of references, having produced or received classified material.

**STANDARD:** Ensuring 100 percent accountability and zero compromise.

**PERFORMANCE STEPS:**
1. Verify classification of materials.
2. Determine the chain of custody procedures for handling sensitive or classified materials.
3. Ensure COMCAM products are marked according to classification.
4. Coordinate destruction of classified material with the Classified Materials Control Coordinator (CMCC).
5. Ensure records are maintained.

**REFERENCES:**
1. DODD 5230.9 Clearance of DoD Information for Public Release
2. MCO 5230.18 Clearance of Department of Defense Information for Public Release
3. MCO 5510.17 Policy for Handling and Safeguarding North Atlantic Treaty Organization (NATO) Material
4. MCO 5510.9 Security of Information for Public Release
5. OPNAVINST 5510.1 Department of the Navy Information and Personnel Security Program Regulation
6. SECNAVINST 5510.30_ Dept of Navy Personnel Security Program
7. Local Standing Operating Procedures (SOP)

---

**4602-MNGT-2011:** Submit lessons learned

**EVALUATION-CODED:** NO          **SUSTAINMENT INTERVAL:** 12 months

**DESCRIPTION:** Marine will write and submit lessons learned.

**MOS PERFORMING:** 4602

**GRADES:** WO-1, CWO-2, CWO-3, CWO-4, CWO-5, CAPT, MAJ, LTCOL

**INITIAL TRAINING SETTING:** FORMAL

**CONDITION:** With the aid of references, given past combat camera operations, a Marine Corps Center for Lessons Learned account, and a CAC enabled computer.

**STANDARD:** Ensuring successes, failures and best practices encountered during combat camera operations are captured.

**PERFORMANCE STEPS:**
1. Review combat camera operations.
2. Compile information for lessons learned report.
3. Edit collected data.
4. Enter data into written lessons learned report.
5. Submit lessons learned report to MCCLL representative.

**REFERENCES:**
1. MCO 3104.1 Marine Corps Combat Camera Program
2. MCO 3504.1 Marine Corps Lessons Learned Program (MCCLP) and the Marine Corps Center for Lessons Learned (MCCLL)
3. SECNAVINST 5216.5 Naval Correspondence Manual
4. Local Standing Operating Procedures (SOP)

---

**4602-MNGT-2012:** Manage COMCAM assets

**EVALUATION-CODED:** NO          **SUSTAINMENT INTERVAL:** 12 months

**DESCRIPTION:** Marine will manage all COMCAM assets including personnel and equipment.

**MOS PERFORMING:** 4602

**GRADES:** WO-1, CWO-2, CWO-3, CWO-4, CWO-5, CAPT, MAJ, LTCOL

**INITIAL TRAINING SETTING:** FORMAL

**CONDITION:** With the aid of references, given a mission and Combat Camera account T/O&E.

**STANDARD:** Ensuring adequate T/O&E allowances are on hand to support the Combat Camera sections mission and in accordance with parent commands procedural guidelines.

**PERFORMANCE STEPS:**
1. Review mission.
2. Determine mission T/O&E requirements.
3. Determine T/O&E excesses/deficiencies.
4. Coordinate the adjustment of the unit T/E through commands S-1/G-1 and S-4/G-4.
5. Review contracts.
6. Draft a statement of work as required.
7. Draft a Table of Organization/Equipment Change Request (TOECR).
8. Reconcile T/O&E changes with OccFld Sponsor/specialist.
9. Draft Universal Needs Statement (UNS) as required.
10. Manage all contracts related to COMCAM.

**REFERENCES:**
1. MCO 3104.1_ Marine Corps Combat Camera Program
2. MCO 3504.1 Marine Corps Lessons Learned Program (MCCLP) and the Marine Corps Center for Lessons Learned (MCCLL)
3. MCO 5311.1_ Total Force Structure Process (TFSP)
4. MCO P4790.2_ MIMMS Field Procedures Manual
5. SECNAVINST 5216.5 Naval Correspondence Manual

---

**4602-MNGT-2013:** Establish imagery movement plan

**EVALUATION-CODED:** NO　　　　**SUSTAINMENT INTERVAL:** 12 months

**DESCRIPTION:** Marine will develop procedures within Operation plan (OPLAN) and Tactical Standard Operating Procedure (TACSOP) that outlines the process.

**MOS PERFORMING:** 4602

**GRADES:** WO-1, CWO-2, CWO-3, CWO-4, CWO-5, CAPT, MAJ, LTCOL

**INITIAL TRAINING SETTING:** FORMAL

**CONDITION:** Given an OPLAN and support mission.

**STANDARD:** Ensuring imagery is moved in accordance with MCO 3104.1B and the local commander's intent.

**PERFORMANCE STEPS:**
1. Review OPLAN.
2. Review TACSOP.
3. Determine available assets.
4. Draft plan.
5. Review plan.
6. Publish plan.

**REFERENCES:**
1. DoDI 5040.07 DoD VI Productions
2. MCO 3104.1_ Marine Corps Combat Camera Program

---

**4602-MNGT-2014**:  Manage a Production

**EVALUATION-CODED**:  NO          **SUSTAINMENT INTERVAL**:  12 months

**DESCRIPTION**:  Marine will manage all requirements of an official Marine Corps motion media production that includes liaison actions between the Office of Primary Responsibility (OPR), possible outside contracts, and all levels of a production.

**MOS PERFORMING**:  4602

**GRADES**:  WO-1, CWO-2, CWO-3, CWO-4, CWO-5, CAPT, MAJ, LTCOL

**INITIAL TRAINING SETTING**:  FORMAL

**CONDITION**:  Given a production requirement, budget, and combat camera assets.

**STANDARD**:  Ensuring production is provided to the OPR that supports the requirement in accordance with DoDI 5040.07.

**PERFORMANCE STEPS**:
1. Determine OPR requirement.
2. Determine level of COMCAM support capable.
3. Assign a project officer.
4. Maintain a production folder.
5. Complete DD Form 1995.
6. Contact the Visual Information Production manager.
7. Provide a copy of the completed production and production folder to the OPR.
8. Forward a digital master of the completed production.

**REFERENCES**:
1. DoDI 5040.07 DoD VI Productions
2. MCO 3104.1B Marine Corps Combat Camera Program

---

**4602-PLAN-2015**:  Direct embarkation of COMCAM equipment

**EVALUATION-CODED**:  NO          **SUSTAINMENT INTERVAL**:  12 months

**MOS PERFORMING**:  4602

**GRADES**:  WO-1, CWO-2, CWO-3, CWO-4, CWO-5, CAPT, MAJ, LTCOL

**INITIAL TRAINING SETTING**:  MOJT

**CONDITION**:  Given a requirement.

**STANDARD**:  Within timeline established by S/G-4.

**PERFORMANCE STEPS**:
1. Identify COMCAM assets required to support mission requirements.
2. Coordinate with command logistics and embarkation representatives (S/G-4).
3. Coordinate TPFDD on Combat Camera assets.

4.  Direct the packing of assets.
5.  Direct equipment inspection/accountability.

**REFERENCES:**
1.  Higher Headquarters OpOrd
2.  Local Standing Operating Procedures (SOP)

---

**4602-PLAN-2016:** Develop the print management program

**EVALUATION-CODED:** NO          **SUSTAINMENT INTERVAL:** 12 months

**DESCRIPTION:** Marine will supervise the print management program to include, but not limited to: needs assessments, technical reviews, copier contracts, and Defense Logistics Agency (DLA) support.

**MOS PERFORMING:** 4602

**GRADES:** WO-1, CWO-2, CWO-3, CWO-4, CWO-5, CAPT, MAJ, LTCOL

**INITIAL TRAINING SETTING:** MOJT

**CONDITION:** Given a local print order.

**STANDARD:** Ensuring the requirement is met, within the time allotted.

**PERFORMANCE STEPS:**
1.  Review requirement.
2.  Review historical data.
3.  Conduct needs assessment; as required.
4.  Conduct technical reviews; as required.
5.  Coordinate with DLA for support; as required.
6.  Monitor contracts.

**REFERENCES:**
1.  MCO 3104.1_ Marine Corps Combat Camera Program
2.  MCO P5600.31_ Marine Corps Publication and Printing Regulations

---

COMCAM T&R MANUAL

## CHAPTER 5

## MOS 4612 INDIVIDUAL EVENTS

CHAPTER 5

MOS 4612 INDIVIDUAL EVENTS

**5000. PURPOSE.** This chapter details the individual events that pertain to MOS 4612, Production Specialist. These events are linked to a service-level Mission Essential Tasks (MET). This linkage tailors individual training for the selected MET. Each individual event provides an event title, along with the conditions events will be performed under, and the standard to which the event must be performed to be successful.

**5001. EVENT CODING.** Events in this T&R Manual are depicted with an up to 12-character, 3-field alphanumeric system, i.e. XXXX-XXXX-XXXX. This chapter utilizes the following methodology:

   a. Field one. This field represents the community. This chapter contains the following community codes:

   | Code | Description |
   |------|-------------|
   | 4612 | Production Specialist |

   b. Field two. This field represents the functional/duty area. This chapter contains the following functional/duty areas:

   | Code | Description |
   |------|-------------|
   | PROD | Production |

   c. Field three. This field provides the level at which the event is accomplished and numerical sequencing of events. This chapter contains the following event levels:

   | Code | Description |
   |------|-------------|
   | 1000 | Core Skills |
   | 2000 | Core Plus Skills |

5002. INDEX OF INDIVIDUAL EVENTS

1. 1000-LEVEL EVENTS

| Event Code | Event | Page |
|---|---|---|
| | PRODUCTION | |
| 4612-PROD-1001 | Create reprographic products | 5-4 |
| 4612-PROD-1002 | Process reprographic products | 5-5 |
| 4612-PROD-1003 | Operate production equipment | 5-5 |
| 4612-PROD-1004 | Conduct post production | 5-6 |
| 4612-PROD-1005 | Conduct print production | 5-7 |
| 4612-PROD-1006 | Process job orders | 5-8 |
| 4612-PROD-1007 | Create production specialist digital portfolio | 5-8 |
| 4612-PROD-1008 | Create original art products | 5-9 |

2. 2000-LEVEL EVENTS

| Event Code | Event | Page |
|---|---|---|
| | PRODUCTION | |
| 4612-PROD-2001 | Maintain production equipment | 5-10 |
| 4612-PROD-2002 | Perform quality control measures | 5-10 |
| 4612-PROD-2003 | Maintain production specialist portfolio | 5-11 |
| 4612-PROD-2004 | Conduct a COMCAM capabilities brief | 5-11 |

5003.  1000-LEVEL EVENTS

**4612-PROD-1001**:  Create reprographic products

**EVALUATION-CODED**:  NO          **SUSTAINMENT INTERVAL**:  12 months

**DESCRIPTION**:  Marine will create products including, but not limited to the following:  finished print products and digital media.

**MOS PERFORMING**:  4612

**GRADES**:  PVT, PFC, LCPL, CPL, SGT, SSGT

**INITIAL TRAINING SETTING**:  FORMAL

**CONDITION**:  In a field environment, with the aid of references, given a Tactical Imagery Production System (TIPS), production workstation, associated software, scanner, and an operational requirement.

**STANDARD**:  Creating a product that meets the operational requirement within a deadline.

**PERFORMANCE STEPS**:
1.  Validate customer requirement.
2.  Log in job order.
3.  Compile media necessary to complete COMCAM product.
4.  Assemble COMCAM product.
5.  Conduct operations/Quality Control check on COMCAM product.
6.  Submit to COMCAM/Production Chief for approval.
7.  Contact requester for proof approval.
8.  Make COMCAM product modifications; as required.
9.  Submit finished COMCAM product to requestor.
10. Archive finished COMCAM product.
11. Complete job order.

**REFERENCES**:
1.  JIEO Report 8307 DOD Guide to Selecting Computer-Based Multimedia Standards, Technologies, Products and Practices
2.  MCO 3104.1_ Marine Corps Combat Camera Program
3.  MCWP 3-33.7 Combat Camera in the MAGTF
4.  TM Technical Manuals
5.  Local Standing Operating Procedures (SOP)

**MISCELLANEOUS**:

  **ADMINISTRATIVE INSTRUCTIONS**:  Multimedia products can include, but are not limited to: command information products in support of information operations, PowerPoint for briefs and/or presentations, computer based training, DVD, CD, MPG, windows and media/real video webpage.

**4612-PROD-1002**: Process reprographic products

**EVALUATION-CODED**: NO          **SUSTAINMENT INTERVAL**: 12 months

**DESCRIPTION**: Marine will ensure that products have assigned VIRINs, contain metadata, are locally archived, contain release information, meet quality control standards and are moved to appropriate archival locations.

**MOS PERFORMING**: 4612

**GRADES**: PVT, PFC, LCPL, CPL, SGT, SSGT

**INITIAL TRAINING SETTING**: FORMAL

**CONDITION**: Given a delivery method, reprographic imagery/media, a production workstation, associated software, and a storage device.

**STANDARD**: Ensuring imagery is processed according to SOP.

**PERFORMANCE STEPS**:
1.  Ensure still imagery is labeled with a VIRIN.
2.  Ensure images are saved in appropriate folder.
3.  Ensure metadata is complete.
4.  Transmit COMCAM product.
5.  Ensure imagery is archived locally.
6.  Ensure imagery is forwarded to appropriate agencies; as required.
7.  Transmit imagery; as required.

**REFERENCES**:
1.  DOD Captioning Style Guide
2.  DOD 5040 Series
3.  DODD 5230.9 Clearance of DOD Information for Public Release
4.  MCO 3104.1_ Marine Corps Combat Camera Program
5.  Local Standing Operating Procedures (SOP)

---

**4612-PROD-1003**: Operate production equipment

**EVALUATION-CODED**: NO          **SUSTAINMENT INTERVAL**: 12 months

**DESCRIPTION**: Marine will operate production equipment including, but not limited to the following: Production workstations, digital production printer, digital media reproduction devices, scanners, finishing and bindery equipment.

**MOS PERFORMING**: 4612

**GRADES**: PVT, PFC, LCPL, CPL, SGT, SSGT

**INITIAL TRAINING SETTING**: FORMAL

**CONDITION**: In a field environment, with the aid of references, given a Tactical Imagery Production System (TIPS), production equipment, safety equipment/guidelines and associated software/materials.

**STANDARD**: Producing products that meet quality assurance standards and in accordance with the references.

**PERFORMANCE STEPS**:
1. Select appropriate equipment needed to accomplish task.
2. Adhere to selected safety equipment/guidelines.
3. Conduct operations check on production equipment.
4. Perform color management.
5. Conduct post operating procedures on production equipment.
6. Perform preventive maintenance as required.

**REFERENCES**:
1. MCO 3104.1_ Marine Corps Combat Camera Program
2. MCWP 3-33.7 Combat Camera in the MAGTF
3. SOP Standard Operating Procedures (SOP)
4. TIPS Manual Tactical Imagery Production System (TIPS) Training Manual
5. TM 10-5411-200-14 Shelter, Tactical, Expandable, Two-Sided (Tactical Imagery Production System)
6. TM 11084A-OI Environmental Control Unit

**MISCELLANEOUS**:

   **ADMINISTRATIVE INSTRUCTIONS**: After initial formal schooling sustainment training of production equipment can be conducted with available reproduction equipment if TIPS is not available at command.

---

**4612-PROD-1004**: Conduct post production

**EVALUATION-CODED**: NO          **SUSTAINMENT INTERVAL**: 12 months

**DESCRIPTION**: Marine will conduct post production which includes, but is not limited to the following: finishing, binding, and mounting.

**MOS PERFORMING**: 4612

**GRADES**: PVT, PFC, LCPL, CPL, SGT, SSGT

**INITIAL TRAINING SETTING**: FORMAL

**CONDITION**: With the aid of references, given production equipment, safety equipment/guidelines, associated materials and a requester's requirement.

**STANDARD**: Within a deadline established by the Standard Operating Procedures (SOP).

**PERFORMANCE STEPS**:
1. Review job order.
2. Select post production equipment/materials.
3. Produce finished product.
4. Conduct quality control check on product.
5. Submit to COMCAM/Production Chief for approval.
6. Make product modifications; as required.
7. Submit finished product to requestor.

8. Archive finished product; as required.
9. Complete job order.

REFERENCES:
1. MCO 3104.1_ Marine Corps Combat Camera Program   •
2. MCO P5600.31_ Marine Corps Publication and Printing Regulations
3. MCWP 3-33.7 Combat Camera in the MAGTF
4. SOP Standard Operating Procedures (SOP)
5. TIPS Manual Tactical Imagery Production System (TIPS) Training Manual
6. TM 10-5411-200-14 Shelter, Tactical, Expandable, Two-Sided (Tactical Imagery Production System)
7. TM 11084A-OI Environmental Control Unit

MISCELLANEOUS:

   ADMINISTRATIVE INSTRUCTIONS: After initial formal schooling sustainment training of production equipment can be conducted with available reproduction equipment if TIPS is not available at command.

---

4612-PROD-1005: Conduct print production

EVALUATION-CODED: NO          SUSTAINMENT INTERVAL: 12 months

DESCRIPTION: Marine will conduct print production which includes printing and duplication.

MOS PERFORMING: 4612

GRADES: PVT, PFC, LCPL, CPL, SGT, SSGT

INITIAL TRAINING SETTING: FORMAL

CONDITION: With the aid of references, given a production workstation, production equipment, safety equipment/guidelines, associated materials and a requester's requirement.

STANDARD: Within a deadline established by the Standard Operating Procedures (SOP).

PERFORMANCE STEPS:
1. Review job order.
2. Select production equipment/materials.
3. Print product.
4. Conduct quality control check on product.
5. Submit to COMCAM/Production Chief for approval.
6. Make product modifications; as required.
7. Submit product for post production.
8. Complete job order.

REFERENCES:
1. MCO 3104.1_ Marine Corps Combat Camera Program
2. MCO P5600.31_ Marine Corps Publication and Printing Regulations
3. MCWP 3-33.7 Combat Camera in the MAGTF

NAVMC 3500.77A
30 Jan 2012

4. SOP Standard Operating Procedures (SOP)
5. TIPS Manual Tactical Imagery Production System (TIPS) Training Manual
6. TM 10-5411-200-14 Shelter, Tactical, Expandable, Two-Sided (Tactical Imagery Production System)
7. TM 11084A-OI Environmental Control Unit

---

**4612-PROD-1006:** Process job orders

**EVALUATION-CODED:** NO          **SUSTAINMENT INTERVAL:** 12 months

**DESCRIPTION:** Marine will utilize the Combat Camera job order database and account for all reprographic products.

**MOS PERFORMING:** 4612

**GRADES:** PVT, PFC, LCPL, CPL, SGT, SSGT

**INITIAL TRAINING SETTING:** FORMAL

**CONDITION:** With the aid of references, given a job order request, CAC enabled production workstation, associated software, and access to the job order database.

**STANDARD:** To account for consumables, man hours, and work units.

**PERFORMANCE STEPS:**
1. Login to the job order database.
2. Create new job request record.
3. Print job request.
4. Obtain customer signature.
5. Route job request to appropriate section.
6. Track job request.
7. File completed job request.

**REFERENCES:**
1. JODUM Job Order Database Users Manual
2. MCO 3104.1 Marine Corps Combat Camera Program
3. SOP Standard Operating Procedures (SOP)

---

**4612-PROD-1007:** Create production specialist digital portfolio

**EVALUATION-CODED:** NO          **SUSTAINMENT INTERVAL:** 12 months

**DESCRIPTION:** Marine will maintain a portfolio that will consist of no less than the following: poster, tri-fold/brochure, leaflet/handbill, Web-page design, and digital illustration.

**MOS PERFORMING:** 4612

**GRADES:** PVT, PFC, LCPL, CPL, SGT, SSGT

INITIAL TRAINING SETTING: FORMAL

CONDITION: Given the reference.

STANDARD: Developing a proper portfolio in accordance with MCO 3104-1B.

PERFORMANCE STEPS:
1. Retrieve COMCAM products.
2. Create portfolio inventory sheet.
3. Assemble portfolio.
4. Create digital media disc.

REFERENCES:
1. MCO 3104.1_ Marine Corps Combat Camera Program

---

4612-PROD-1008: Create original art products

EVALUATION-CODED: NO          SUSTAINMENT INTERVAL: 12 months

DESCRIPTION: Marine will develop COMCAM products including, but not limited to; fine art and digital graphic designs.

MOS PERFORMING: 4612

GRADES: PVT, PFC, LCPL, CPL, SGT, SSGT

INITIAL TRAINING SETTING: FORMAL

CONDITION: Given artistic tools or a production workstation, associated media or software, scanner, and an operational requirement.

STANDARD: Creating a COMCAM product that meets the operational requirement.

PERFORMANCE STEPS:
1. Validate operational requirement.
2. Log in job order.
3. Compile media necessary to complete product.
4. Select graphic style to meet requirement.
5. Develop graphic art product.
6. Submit to COMCAM/Production Chief for approval.
7. Contact requester for proof approval.
8. Make product modifications; as required.
9. Submit finished product to requestor.
10. Archive finished product.
11. Complete job order.

REFERENCES:
1. MCO 3104.1_ Marine Corps Combat Camera Program
2. MCWP 3-33.7 Combat Camera in the MAGTF
3. OPNAVINST 5040.4_ Navy Insignia
4. SOP Standard Operating Procedures (SOP)

5004. 2000-LEVEL EVENTS

4612-PROD-2001: Maintain production equipment

EVALUATION-CODED: NO          SUSTAINMENT INTERVAL: 12 months

DESCRIPTION: Marine will ensure that functional inspections are conducted as required in order to ensure equipment is operational. Production equipment includes, but is not limited to the following: reprographic equipment.

MOS PERFORMING: 4612

GRADES: CPL, SGT, SSGT

INITIAL TRAINING SETTING: MOJT

CONDITION: Given a Tactical Imagery Production System (TIPS) or production equipment, trouble shooting log and maintenance tools.

STANDARD: Ensuring all systems are operational.

PERFORMANCE STEPS:
1. Conduct operations check on systems.
2. Troubleshoot errors.
3. Correct error/malfunction.
4. Identify unserviceable equipment and or components.
5. Take corrective measures to repair or replace.
6. Maintain preventative maintenance jacket.

REFERENCES:
1. MCO 4790.7 Marine Corps Integrated Maintenance Management System Automated Information System, Headquarters Maintenance Subsystem, Headquarters Users Manual (Aug 77)
2. SOP Standard Operating Procedures (SOP)

MISCELLANEOUS:

ADMINISTRATIVE INSTRUCTIONS: Authorize maintenance will be determined according to service contract.

4612-PROD-2002: Perform quality control measures

EVALUATION-CODED: NO          SUSTAINMENT INTERVAL: 12 months

DESCRIPTION: Marine will perform quality control standards to meet operational requirements.

MOS PERFORMING: 4612

GRADES: CPL, SGT, SSGT

INITIAL TRAINING SETTING: MOJT

CONDITION: With the aid of references.

STANDARD: Ensuring the product meets operational requirements.

PERFORMANCE STEPS:
1. Review job order.
2. Review the product.
3. Ensure approved requirements are met.
4. Repeat steps 1 thru 3; as required.

REFERENCES:
1. DOD Captioning Style Guide
2. MCO 3104.1_ Marine Corps Combat Camera Program
3. MCO P5600.31_ Marine Corps Publication and Printing Regulations
4. SOP Standard Operating Procedures (SOP)

---

4612-PROD-2003: Maintain production specialist portfolio

EVALUATION-CODED: NO          SUSTAINMENT INTERVAL: 12 months

DESCRIPTION: Marine will maintain a portfolio that will consist of no less than the following: Poster, Tri-fold/brochure, leaflet/handbill, Web-page design, digital illustration, publication, collated and bound product, and interactive multi-media product.

MOS PERFORMING: 4612

GRADES: PVT, PFC, LCPL, CPL, SGT, SSGT

INITIAL TRAINING SETTING: MOJT

CONDITION: With the aid of reference, given COMCAM products, production equipment, production workstation, and associated software.

STANDARD: Maintaining a portfolio in accordance with MCO 3104.1B.

PERFORMANCE STEPS:
1. Update COMCAM products.
2. Update portfolio inventory sheet.
3. Assemble portfolio.
4. Create digital media disc.
5. Print portfolio; as required.

REFERENCES:
1. MCO 3104.1_ Marine Corps Combat Camera Program

---

4612-PROD-2004: Conduct a COMCAM capabilities brief

EVALUATION-CODED: NO          SUSTAINMENT INTERVAL: 12 months

**DESCRIPTION**: Marine will conduct a COMCAM Capabilities Brief in order to educate target audience on the capabilities and limitations of Marine Combat Camera which will assist in the proper employment of COMCAM assets.

**MOS PERFORMING**: 4612

**GRADES**: SSGT

**INITIAL TRAINING SETTING**: MOJT

**CONDITION**: Given a requirement, a production work station, briefing format, briefing materials, and a target audience.

**STANDARD**: Ensuring COMCAM capabilities and limitations are fully explained in accordance with Marine Corps Combat Camera Program.

**PERFORMANCE STEPS**:
1. Review the references.
2. Prepare the brief.
3. Prepare handouts; as required.
4. Rehearse the brief.

**REFERENCES**:
1. MCO 3104.1_ Marine Corps Combat Camera Program
2. MCWP 3-33.7 Combat Camera in the MAGTF
3. SOP Standard Operating Procedures (SOP)

COMCAM T&R MANUAL

CHAPTER 6

MOS 4641 INDIVIDUAL EVENTS

COMCAM T&R MANUAL

CHAPTER 6

MOS 4641 INDIVIDUAL EVENTS

**6000. PURPOSE.** This chapter details the individual events that pertain to MOS 4641, Combat Photographer. These events are linked to a service-level Mission Essential Tasks (MET). This linkage tailor's individual training for the selected MET. Each individual event provides an event title, along with the conditions events will be performed under, and the standard to which the event must be performed to be successful.

**6001. EVENT CODING.** Events in this T&R Manual are depicted with an up to 12-character, 3-field alphanumeric system, i.e. XXXX-XXXX-XXXX. This chapter utilizes the following methodology:

a. Field one. This field represents the community. This chapter contains the following community codes:

| Code | Description |
|------|-------------|
| 4641 | Combat Photographer |

b. Field two. This field represents the functional/duty area. This chapter contains the following functional/duty areas:

| Code | Description |
|------|-------------|
| PHTO | Photography |

c. Field three. This field provides the level at which the event is accomplished and numerical sequencing of events. This chapter contains the following event levels:

| Code | Description |
|------|-------------|
| 1000 | Core Skills |
| 2000 | Core Plus Skills |

6002. INDEX OF INDIVIDUAL EVENTS

1. 1000-LEVEL EVENTS

| Event Code | Event | Page |
|---|---|---|
| | PHOTOGRAPHY | |
| 4641-PHTO-1001 | Edit still imagery | 6-4 |
| 4641-PHTO-1002 | Caption still images (metadata) | 6-4 |
| 4641-PHTO-1003 | Archive still imagery | 6-5 |
| 4641-PHTO-1004 | Process still imagery products | 6-6 |
| 4641-PHTO-1005 | Capture still images in an operational environment | 6-6 |
| 4641-PHTO-1006 | Capture still images in an administrative environment | 6-7 |
| 4641-PHTO-1007 | Conduct still documentation of an sensitive site | 6-8 |
| 4641-PHTO-1008 | Develop photographic products | 6-9 |
| 4641-PHTO-1009 | Operate photographic production equipment | 6-10 |
| 4641-PHTO-1010 | Create a still photographic digital portfolio | 6-11 |

2. 2000-LEVEL EVENTS

| Event Code | Event | Page |
|---|---|---|
| | PHOTOGRAPHY | |
| 4641-PHTO-2001 | Maintain photographic equipment | 6-13 |
| 4641-PHTO-2002 | Maintain a still photographic portfolio | 6-13 |
| 4641-PHTO-2003 | Conduct a COMCAM capabilities brief | 6-14 |

**6003. 1000-LEVEL EVENTS**

**4641-PHTO-1001:** Edit still imagery

**EVALUATION-CODED:** NO      **SUSTAINMENT INTERVAL:** 12 months

**DESCRIPTION:** Marine will edit imagery by selecting specific or requested imagery, the removal of redundant and unusable (out of focus, improper exposure, improper composition, inappropriate content) photographs. Editing also includes properly naming (VIRIN).

**MOS PERFORMING:** 4641

**BILLETS:** Combat Photographer

**GRADES:** PVT, PFC, LCPL, CPL, SGT, SSGT

**INITIAL TRAINING SETTING:** FORMAL

**CONDITION:** Given a requirement, captured still imagery, Visual Information Imagery Editing System (VIIES), associated software and a storage device.

**STANDARD:** Producing a final product that meets the requirement within a deadline established by the SOP.

**PERFORMANCE STEPS:**
1. View images.
2. Select required images.
3. Save selected images as Visual Information Record and Identification Number (VIRIN).

**REFERENCES:**
1. DODD 5040.5 Alteration of Official DoD Imagery
2. DODD 5230.9 Clearance of DoD Information for Public Release
3. MCO 3104.1_ Marine Corps Combat Camera Program
4. MCWP 3-33.7 Combat Camera in the MAGTF
5. Local Standing Operating Procedures (SOP)

---

**4641-PHTO-1002:** Caption still images (metadata)

**EVALUATION-CODED:** NO      **SUSTAINMENT INTERVAL:** 12 months

**DESCRIPTION:** Marine will caption imagery by providing all DoD required metadata to include; caption, operation/exercise name, photographers rank/name, photographers home unit, photographers TDY unit, VIRIN, image source, captioned editor, base/local, state/province, county/area, date shot, command shown, service shown, supplemental category, public release instruction, and key words.

**MOS PERFORMING:** 4641

**BILLETS:** Combat Photographer

GRADES: PVT, PFC, LCPL, CPL, SGT, SSGT

INITIAL TRAINING SETTING: FORMAL

CONDITION: Given captured still imagery, caption data, a Visual Information Imagery Editing System (VIIES), and associated software.

STANDARD: Ensuring all DoD required metadata is included, within a deadline established by the SOP.

PERFORMANCE STEPS:
1. Review gathered caption data.
2. Complete metadata.
3. Save image using VIRIN naming convention.
4. Edit caption for accuracy, spelling, and grammar.
5. Submit to caption editor for review.
6. Correct metadata; as required.

REFERENCES:
1. DOD Style Guide
2. DOD 5040 Series
3. JCS PUB 1-02 DoD Dictionary of Military and Associated Terms
4. MCO 3104.1_ Marine Corps Combat Camera Program
5. Operator's Manual Operator's Manual
6. SOP Standard Operating Procedures (SOP)
7. VIIES Visual Information Imagery Editing System Operators Manual

---

**4641-PHTO-1003**: Archive still imagery

EVALUATION-CODED: NO                SUSTAINMENT INTERVAL: 12 months

DESCRIPTION: Marine will archive imagery for future requirements and historical purposes.

MOS PERFORMING: 4641

BILLETS: Combat Photographer

GRADES: PVT, PFC, LCPL, CPL, SGT, SSGT

INITIAL TRAINING SETTING: FORMAL

CONDITION: In a field environment, given digital imagery, a production workstation, associated software, and a storage device.

STANDARD: Ensuring that images archived contain complete and accurate metadata in accordance with the references.

PERFORMANCE STEPS:
1. Review metadata.
2. Save image.

REFERENCES:
1.  DOD Style Guide
2.  DOD 5040 Series
3.  SOP Standard Operating Procedures (SOP)

MISCELLANEOUS:

ADMINISTRATIVE INSTRUCTIONS:  Archive media may consist of, but not limited to; Compact Disk (CD), Digital Versatile Disk (DVD), Media Server Storage (Database, Web base).  Archived imagery should be in raw form and always duplicated in effort in order to ensure loss of data doesn't occur.  Multiple archives ensure data can be retrieved in case one becomes lost and not retrievable.

---

4641-PHTO-1004:  Process still imagery products

EVALUATION-CODED:  NO          SUSTAINMENT INTERVAL:  12 months

MOS PERFORMING:  4641

GRADES:  PVT, PFC, LCPL, CPL, SGT, SSGT

INITIAL TRAINING SETTING:  FORMAL

CONDITION:  In a field environment, with the aid of references, given still imagery, a Visual Information Imagery Editing System (VIIES), associated software, and a storage device.

STANDARD:  Ensuring imagery is processed according to Standard Operating Procedures (SOP).

PERFORMANCE STEPS:
1.  Ensure still imagery is labeled with a VIRIN.
2.  Ensure labeled images are saved in appropriate folder with the VIRIN naming convention (071231-M-1234S).
3.  Ensure metadata is complete and accurate.
4.  Ensure still imagery contains releasing classification.
5.  Ensure imagery is archived locally.
6.  Ensure imagery is forwarded to appropriate agencies; as required.
7.  Transmit imagery; as required.

REFERENCES:
1.  DOD Style Guide
2.  DOD 5040 Series
3.  DODD 5230.9 Clearance of DoD Information for Public Release
4.  MCO 3104.1_ Marine Corps Combat Camera Program
5.  SOP Standard Operating Procedures (SOP)

---

4641-PHTO-1005:  Capture still images in an operational environment

EVALUATION-CODED:  NO          SUSTAINMENT INTERVAL:  12 months

DESCRIPTION: Marine will capture still images in an operational environment consisting of but not limited to the following: taking still images during combat operations, exercises, and training. This event must be performed in full light, low light and no-light conditions.

MOS PERFORMING: 4641

BILLETS: Combat Photographer

GRADES: PVT, PFC, LCPL, CPL, SGT, SSGT

INITIAL TRAINING SETTING: FORMAL

CONDITION: Using a Combat Still Acquisition System (CSAS), Night Vision System (NVS), T/O weapon, combat load, and a requirement.

STANDARD: Acquiring still imagery that meets the requirement.

PERFORMANCE STEPS:
1. Review requirement.
2. Coordinate support with requestor; as required.
3. Select required equipment.
4. Acclimatize equipment for weather conditions.
5. Conduct equipment operations check.
6. Select camera/flash settings.
7. Compose and focus image.
8. Capture image.
9. Gather caption data.

REFERENCES:
1. MCWP 3-33.7 Combat Camera in the MAGTF
2. Operator's Manual Operator's Manual
3. Local Standing Operating Procedures (SOP)
4. Operations Order

---

**4641-PHTO-1006:** Capture still images in an administrative environment

EVALUATION-CODED: NO                SUSTAINMENT INTERVAL: 12 months

DESCRIPTION: Marine will capture images in an administrative environment consisting of but not limited to the following: studio (command portraits, promotion, passport, and still life photographs), command information, ceremonial (changes of command and post and relief, retirements and awards).

MOS PERFORMING: 4641

BILLETS: Combat Photographer

GRADES: PVT, PFC, LCPL, CPL, SGT, SSGT

INITIAL TRAINING SETTING: FORMAL

CONDITION: Given a still acquisition kit, specialized equipment, and a requirement.

STANDARD: Acquiring still imagery that meets the requirement.

PERFORMANCE STEPS:
1. Review requirement.
2. Coordinate support with requestor; as required.
3. Select appropriate equipment needed to complete mission.
4. Acclimatize equipment for weather conditions.
5. Conduct equipment operations check.
6. Select camera/flash settings.
7. Compose and focus image.
8. Capture image.
9. Gather caption data; as required.
10. Transmit images; as required.

REFERENCES:
1. MCO 3104.1_ Marine Corps Combat Camera Program
2. MCO 5512.4_ No-fee Passports
3. MCO P1070.12_ Marine Corps Individual Records Administration Manual (IRAM)
4. Operator's Manual
5. SOP Standard Operating Procedures (SOP)

MISCELLANEOUS:

ADMINISTRATIVE INSTRUCTIONS: Specialized equipment consists of macro lenses, micro lenses, ring flash, filters, studio lighting, standards, colors, and backdrops.

---

4641-PHTO-1007: Conduct still documentation of a sensitive site

EVALUATION-CODED: NO          SUSTAINMENT INTERVAL: 12 months

DESCRIPTION: Marine will capture still images of a scene consisting of but not limited to the following types: forensic, mishap, crime and tactical/sensitive sites.

MOS PERFORMING: 4641

GRADES: PVT, PFC, LCPL, CPL, SGT, SSGT

INITIAL TRAINING SETTING: FORMAL

CONDITION: Given a still acquisition kit, specialized equipment, night vision kit (SL3 complete), and a requirement.

STANDARD: Acquiring still imagery that focuses on the identifying details of a site and meets the requirement and in accordance with the references.

PERFORMANCE STEPS:
1. Review requirement.
2. Select required equipment.

3.  Acclimatize equipment for weather conditions.
4.  Conduct equipment operations check.
5.  Coordinate with investigative representative/on scene commander for access to site and imagery requirements.
6.  Photograph establishing shot of site at multiple angles.
7.  Photograph site in panoramic covering 360 degrees (outside to inside).
8.  Photograph detailed evidence established by investigating official with ruler or other object in site to determine scale.
9.  Gather caption data.
10. Caption imagery; as required.
11. Label photos in accordance with classification guidance from investigating official.
12. Establish chain of custody as required.
13. Archive imagery; as required.

**REFERENCES:**
1.  DOD Style Guide
2.  DODD 5230.9 Clearance of DoD Information for Public Release
3.  JCS PUB 1-02 DoD Dictionary of Military and Associated Terms
4.  Operator's Manual Operator's Manual
5.  SOP Standard Operating Procedures (SOP)

**MISCELLANEOUS:**

**ADMINISTRATIVE INSTRUCTIONS:**  Sensitive site examples are enemy weapon caches, mass graves, torture chambers, POW sites, WMD sites, Improvised Explosive Device (IED) sites, enemy use of protected sites (hospitals, religious buildings, schools etc.)  Examples of forensic photography include autopsy, aircraft mishap, vehicle mishap, suicide, material deficiency reports, crime scene etc...  Examples of scale may include any common item (ruler, pen, ID card, boot, person) that is placed near or next to item being photographed for reference of size.  Specialized equipment consists of macro lenses, micro lenses, ring flash, filters, color scale, and slate.  Do not erase any still imagery acquired in support of an official investigation.

---

**4641-PHTO-1008:**  Develop photographic products

**EVALUATION-CODED:**  NO            **SUSTAINMENT INTERVAL:**  12 months

**DESCRIPTION:**  Marine will develop products including, but not limited to: photographic layouts, print media, digital media to include multimedia presentations and web based products.

**MOS PERFORMING:**  4641

**BILLETS:**  Combat Photographer

**GRADES:**  PVT, PFC, LCPL, CPL, SGT, SSGT

**INITIAL TRAINING SETTING:**  FORMAL

CONDITION: In a field environment, given a Tactical Imagery Production System (TIPS), a production workstation, associated software, production equipment, and an operational requirement.

STANDARD: Creating a photographic product that meets the operational requirement.

PERFORMANCE STEPS:
1. Validate customer requirement.
2. Log in job order.
3. Compile media necessary to complete product.
4. Assemble product.
5. Conduct operations/quality control check on product.
6. Submit to COMCAM/Production Chief for approval.
7. Contact requester for proof approval.
8. Make product modifications; as required.
9. Submit finished product to requestor.
10. Archive finished product.
11. Complete job order.

REFERENCES:
1. MCO 3104.1_ Marine Corps Combat Camera Program
2. SOP Standard Operating Procedures (SOP)
3. TIPS Manual Tactical Imagery Production System (TIPS) Training Manual
4. TM 10-5411-200-14 Shelter, Tactical, Expandable, Two-Sided (Tactical Imagery Production System)
5. TM 11084A-OI Environmental Control Unit

MISCELLANEOUS:

ADMINISTRATIVE INSTRUCTIONS: Multimedia products can include, but are not limited to: command information products in support of information operations and MISO, PowerPoint for briefs and/or presentations Computer Based Training/DVD/VCD/MPG/Windows Media/Real Video Webpage

---

4641-PHTO-1009: Operate photographic production equipment

EVALUATION-CODED: NO          SUSTAINMENT INTERVAL: 12 months

DESCRIPTION: Marine will operate photographic production equipment including, but not limited to the following: Production workstations, printers, digital media reproduction devices and scanners.

MOS PERFORMING: 4641

BILLETS: Combat Photographer

GRADES: PVT, PFC, LCPL, CPL, SGT, SSGT

INITIAL TRAINING SETTING: FORMAL

CONDITION: In a field environment, given a Tactical Imagery Production System (TIPS), production equipment, a production workstation, and associated software.

STANDARD: Producing products that meet quality control standards.

PERFORMANCE STEPS:
1. Select appropriate equipment.
2. Conduct operations check on production equipment.
3. Perform color management.
4. Conduct post operating procedures on production equipment.
5. Perform preventive maintenance as required.

REFERENCES:
1. MCO 3104.1_ Marine Corps Combat Camera Program
2. MCWP 3-33.7 Combat Camera in the MAGTF
3. SOP Standard Operating Procedures (SOP)
4. TIPS Manual Tactical Imagery Production System (TIPS) Training Manual
5. TM 10-5411-200-14 Shelter, Tactical, Expandable, Two-Sided (Tactical Imagery Production System)
6. TM 11084A-OI Environmental Control Unit
7. SL-3-4120 Family of Environmental Control Units
8. SL-3-6115 Generator Set, Diesel Engine Driven, Skid Mounted

---

**4641-PHTO-1010:** Create a still photographic digital portfolio

EVALUATION-CODED: NO          SUSTAINMENT INTERVAL: 12 months

MOS PERFORMING: 4641

BILLETS: Combat Photographer

GRADES: PVT, PFC, LCPL

INITIAL TRAINING SETTING: FORMAL

CONDITION: Using still imagery, a production workstation, and associated software.

STANDARD: Producing a portfolio in accordance with Marine Corps Combat Camera Program.

PERFORMANCE STEPS:
1. Retrieve developed products.
2. Create portfolio inventory sheet.
3. Create digital media disc.

REFERENCES:
1. MCO 3104.1_ Marine Corps Combat Camera Program

**MISCELLANEOUS**:

    **ADMINISTRATIVE INSTRUCTIONS**: Operational support includes, but is not
limited to: (IO, BDA, CMO, HumOps, Intel, PsyOp, PA, Forensics)

---

6004.  2000-LEVEL EVENTS

**4641-PHTO-2001**:  Maintain photographic equipment

**EVALUATION-CODED**:  NO            **SUSTAINMENT INTERVAL**:  12 months

**DESCRIPTION**:  Marine will ensure that functional inspections are conducted on a regular basis in order to ensure equipment is combat ready.  Photographic equipment includes, but is not limited to the following:  photographic printers, cameras, lenses, flashes, lighting, and tripods.

**MOS PERFORMING**:  4641

**BILLETS**:  Combat Photographer

**GRADES**:  PVT, PFC, LCPL, CPL, SGT, SSGT

**INITIAL TRAINING SETTING**:  FORMAL

**CONDITION**:  Given photographic equipment, trouble shooting log and maintenance tools.

**STANDARD**:  Ensuring all systems are operational.

**PERFORMANCE STEPS**:
1.  Conduct operations check on systems.
2.  Troubleshoot errors.
3.  Correct error/malfunction.
4.  Identify unserviceable equipment and or components.
5.  Take corrective measures to repair or replace.
6.  Maintain preventative maintenance jacket.

**REFERENCES**:
1.  AEOM Appropriate equipment owner's manual
2.  SOP Standard Operating Procedures (SOP)
3.  TM Technical Manuals

---

**4641-PHTO-2002**:  Maintain a still photographic portfolio

**EVALUATION-CODED**:  NO            **SUSTAINMENT INTERVAL**:  12 months

**MOS PERFORMING**:  4641

**BILLETS**:  Combat Photographer

**GRADES**:  PVT, PFC, LCPL, CPL, SGT, SSGT

**INITIAL TRAINING SETTING**:  MOJT

**CONDITION**:  With the aid of reference, given captured imagery, photographic equipment, and workstation and associated software.

STANDARD: Maintaining a portfolio in accordance with Marine Corps Combat Camera Program.

PERFORMANCE STEPS:
1. Determine portfolio requirements.
2. Update products.
3. Update portfolio inventory sheet.
4. Create digital media disc.
5. Print portfolio; as required.

REFERENCES:
1. MCO 3104.1_ Marine Corps Combat Camera Program

---

**4641-PHTO-2003**: Conduct a COMCAM capabilities brief

EVALUATION-CODED: NO          SUSTAINMENT INTERVAL: 12 months

DESCRIPTION: Marine will conduct a COMCAM capabilities brief in order to educate target audience on the capabilities and limitations of Marine Combat Camera which will assist in the proper employment of COMCAM assets.

MOS PERFORMING: 4641

BILLETS: Combat Photographer

GRADES: SSGT

INITIAL TRAINING SETTING: MOJT

CONDITION: Given a requirement, a production work station, briefing format, briefing materials, and a target audience.

STANDARD: Ensuring COMCAM capabilities and limitations are fully explained, within the time allotted and in accordance with Marine Corps Combat Camera Program.

PERFORMANCE STEPS:
1. Review the references.
2. Prepare the brief.
3. Prepare handouts; as required.
4. Rehearse the brief.
5. Conduct the brief.
6. Answer questions.

REFERENCES:
1. MCO 3104.1_ Marine Corps Combat Camera Program
2. MCWP 3-33.7 Combat Camera in the MAGTF
3. Local Standing Operating Procedures (SOP)

---

COMCAM T&R MANUAL

CHAPTER 7

MOS 4671 INDIVIDUAL EVENTS

COMCAM T&R MANUAL

CHAPTER 7

MOS 4671 INDIVIDUAL EVENTS

**7000. PURPOSE.** This chapter details the individual events that pertain to MOS 4671, Combat Videographer. These events are linked to a service-level Mission Essential Tasks (MET). This linkage tailor's individual training for the selected MET. Each individual event provides an event title, along with the conditions events will be performed under, and the standard to which the event must be performed to be successful.

**7001. EVENT CODING.** Events in this T&R Manual are depicted with an up to 12-character, 3-field alphanumeric system, i.e. XXXX-XXXX-XXXX. This chapter utilizes the following methodology:

a. Field one. This field represents the community. This chapter contains the following community codes:

| Code | Description |
|------|-------------|
| 4671 | Combat Videographer |

b. Field two. This field represents the functional/duty area. This chapter contains the following functional/duty areas:

| Code | Description |
|------|-------------|
| VIDS | Videography |

c. Field three. This field provides the level at which the event is accomplished and numerical sequencing of events. This chapter contains the following event levels:

| Code | Description |
|------|-------------|
| 1000 | Core Skills |
| 2000 | Core Plus Skills |

7002. INDEX OF INDIVIDUAL EVENTS

1. 1000-LEVEL EVENTS

| Event Code | Event | Page |
|---|---|---|
| | VIDEOGRAPHY | |
| 4671-VIDS-1001 | Develop prime cuts | 7-4 |
| 4671-VIDS-1002 | Caption motion media (metadata) | 7-4 |
| 4671-VIDS-1003 | Archive motion media | 7-5 |
| 4671-VIDS-1004 | Process motion media products | 7-6 |
| 4671-VIDS-1005 | Capture motion media in an operational environment | 7-7 |
| 4671-VIDS-1006 | Capture motion media in an administrative environment | 7-7 |
| 4671-VIDS-1007 | Conduct motion media documentation of a sensitive site | 7-8 |
| 4671-VIDS-1008 | Develop motion media products | 7-9 |
| 4671-VIDS-1009 | Operate production equipment | 7-10 |
| 4671-VIDS-1010 | Create a motion media digital portfolio | 7-11 |
| 4671-VIDS-1011 | Conduct motion media pre-production | 7-11 |
| 4671-VIDS-1012 | Conduct a motion media production | 7-12 |
| 4671-VIDS-1013 | Conduct motion media post-production | 7-13 |

2. 2000-LEVEL EVENTS

| Event Code | Event | Page |
|---|---|---|
| | VIDEOGRAPHY | |
| 4671-VIDS-2001 | Maintain motion media equipment | 7-14 |
| 4671-VIDS-2002 | Maintain a motion media portfolio | 7-14 |
| 4671-VIDS-2003 | Conduct a COMCAM capabilities brief | 7-15 |

**7003. 1000-LEVEL EVENTS**

**4671-VIDS-1001:** Develop prime cuts

**EVALUATION-CODED:** NO          **SUSTAINMENT INTERVAL:** 12 months

**DESCRIPTION:** Marine will develop prime cuts consisting of motion imagery used in follow on motion media products.

**MOS PERFORMING:** 4671

**GRADES:** PVT, PFC, LCPL, CPL, SGT, SSGT

**INITIAL TRAINING SETTING:** FORMAL

**CONDITION:** In a field environment, given an operational requirement, DD Form 2537, captured motion media, a Visual Information Imagery Editing System (VIIES), associated software, and a storage device.

**STANDARD:** Creating a motion media product that meets the requirement.

**PERFORMANCE STEPS:**
1. Review motion media.
2. Create edit decision list, EDL.
3. Assemble edit prime cuts using EDL.
4. Create slate.
5. Create DD Form 2537 (Caption Sheet).
6. Insert metadata.
7. Output prime cuts to selected medium.
8. Save selected prime cut as Visual Information Record Identification Number (VIRIN).

**REFERENCES:**
1. DOD Captioning Style Guide
2. DODD 5040.5 Alteration of Official DoD Imagery
3. DODD 5230.9 Clearance of DoD Information for Public Release
4. MCO 3104.1_ Marine Corps Combat Camera Program
5. MCWP 3-33.7 Combat Camera in the MAGTF
6. SOP Standard Operating Procedures (SOP)

---

**4671-VIDS-1002:** Caption motion media (metadata)

**EVALUATION-CODED:** NO          **SUSTAINMENT INTERVAL:** 12 months

**DESCRIPTION:** Marine will caption motion media by providing all DoD required metadata to include; description, title, photographer, VIRIN, captioned editor, date shot, public release instruction, and key words.

**MOS PERFORMING:** 4671

**GRADES:** PVT, PFC, LCPL, CPL, SGT, SSGT

INITIAL TRAINING SETTING: FORMAL

CONDITION: In a field environment, given motion media, caption data, a Visual Information Imagery Editing System (VIIES), associated software, and a storage device.

STANDARD: Ensuring all required metadata is included within a deadline established by the Standard Operating Procedures (SOP).

PERFORMANCE STEPS:
1. Review gathered caption data.
2. Complete DD Form 2537.
3. Submit to caption editor for review.
4. Correct metadata; as required.
5. Complete metadata.
6. Save motion media using VIRIN naming convention.

REFERENCES:
1. DOD Captioning Style Guide
2. DOD 5040 Series
3. JCS PUB 1-02 DoD Dictionary of Military and Associated Terms
4. MCO 3104.1_ Marine Corps Combat Camera Program
5. SOP Standard Operating Procedures (SOP)
6. VIIES Visual Information Imagery Editing System Operators Manual

---

4671-VIDS-1003: Archive motion media

EVALUATION-CODED: NO          SUSTAINMENT INTERVAL: 12 months

DESCRIPTION: Marines will archive motion media for future requirements and historical purposes.

MOS PERFORMING: 4671

GRADES: PVT, PFC, LCPL, CPL, SGT, SSGT

INITIAL TRAINING SETTING: FORMAL

CONDITION: In a field environment, given a Tactical Imagery Production System (TIPS), motion media, a production workstation, associated software, and a storage device.

STANDARD: Ensuring motion media archived contains a completed DD Form 2537 and valid metadata.

PERFORMANCE STEPS:
1. Review motion media.
2. Review metadata.
3. Save DD Form 2537.
4. Save motion media to local archive.

REFERENCES:
1. DOD Captioning Style Guide

2. DOD 5040 Series
3. MCO 3104.1_ Marine Corps Combat Camera Program
4. SOP Standard Operating Procedures (SOP)

**MISCELLANEOUS:**

**ADMINISTRATIVE INSTRUCTIONS:** Archive media may consist of, but not limited to; Compact Disk (CD), Digital Versatile Disk (DVD), Media Server Storage (Database, Web base). Archived imagery should be in raw form and always duplicated in effort in order to ensure loss of data doesn't occur. Multiple archives ensure data can be retrieved in case one becomes lost and irretrievable.

---

**4671-VIDS-1004:** Process motion media products

**EVALUATION-CODED:** NO          **SUSTAINMENT INTERVAL:** 12 months

**DESCRIPTION:** Marine will ensure that products have assigned VIRINs, contain metadata, a completed DD Form 2537, are locally archived, contain release information, meet quality control standards and are transmitted.

**MOS PERFORMING:** 4671

**GRADES:** PVT, PFC, LCPL, CPL, SGT, SSGT

**INITIAL TRAINING SETTING:** FORMAL

**CONDITION:** In a field environment, given motion media, a Visual Information Imagery Editing System (VIIES), associated software, and a storage device.

**STANDARD:** In performance step sequence, to ensure products are processed, in accordance with the references.

**PERFORMANCE STEPS:**
1. Ensure motion media is labeled with a VIRIN.
2. Ensure motion media is saved in appropriate folder.
3. Ensure DD Form 2537 is complete.
4. Ensure metadata is complete.
5. Ensure motion media contains releasing classification.
6. Ensure motion media is archived locally.
7. Ensure motion media is forwarded to appropriate agencies; as required.
8. Transmit motion media; as required.

**REFERENCES:**
1. DOD Captioning Style Guide
2. DOD 5040 Series
3. DODD 5230.9 Clearance of DoD Information for Public Release
4. MCO 3104.1_ Marine Corps Combat Camera Program
5. SOP Standard Operating Procedures (SOP)

---

**4671-VIDS-1005:** Capture motion media in an operational environment

**EVALUATION-CODED:** NO          **SUSTAINMENT INTERVAL:** 12 months

**DESCRIPTION:** Marine will capture motion media in an operational environment consisting of but not limited to the following:  acquiring motion media during operations, exercises, and training.

**MOS PERFORMING:** 4671

**GRADES:** PVT, PFC, LCPL, CPL, SGT, SSGT

**INITIAL TRAINING SETTING:** FORMAL

**CONDITION:** Using a Combat Video Acquisition System (CVAS), Night Vision System (NVS), T/O weapon, combat load, and a requirement.

**STANDARD:** Acquiring motion media that meets the requirement.

**PERFORMANCE STEPS:**
1. Review requirement.
2. Coordinate support with requestor; as required.
3. Select required equipment.
4. Acclimatize equipment for weather conditions
5. Conduct equipment operations check.
6. Select camera settings.
7. Compose and focus image.
8. Capture motion media.
9. Gather caption data.

**REFERENCES:**
1. MCWP 3-33.7 Combat Camera in the MAGTF
2. Operator's Manual
3. SOP Standard Operating Procedures (SOP)
4. TPH Television Production Handbook, Current Edition, Zettl, Herbert
5. Operations Order

---

**4671-VIDS-1006:** Capture motion media in an administrative environment

**EVALUATION-CODED:** NO          **SUSTAINMENT INTERVAL:** 12 months

**DESCRIPTION:** Marine will capture motion media in an administrative environment consisting of but not limited to the following:  Studio, command information, ceremonial.

**MOS PERFORMING:** 4671

**GRADES:** PVT, PFC, LCPL, CPL, SGT, SSGT

**INITIAL TRAINING SETTING:** FORMAL

**CONDITION:** Given a video acquisition kit, specialized equipment, and a requirement.

**STANDARD:** Acquiring motion media that meets the requirement.

**PERFORMANCE STEPS:**
1. Review requirement.
2. Coordinate support with requestor; as required.
3. Select appropriate equipment needed to complete mission.
4. Acclimatize equipment for weather conditions.
5. Conduct equipment operations check.
6. Select camera/lighting settings.
7. Gather caption data; as required.
8. Transmit motion media; as required.

**REFERENCES:**
1. MCO 3104.1_ Marine Corps Combat Camera Program
2. Operator's Manual Operator's Manual
3. SOP Standard Operating Procedures (SOP)
4. TPH Television Production Handbook, Current Edition, Zettl, Herbert

**MISCELLANEOUS:**

   **ADMINISTRATIVE INSTRUCTIONS:** Specialized equipment consists of filters, studio lighting, standards, colors, microphones, teleprompters, audio booth, and backdrops.

---

**4671-VIDS-1007:** Conduct motion media documentation of a sensitive site

**EVALUATION-CODED:** NO          **SUSTAINMENT INTERVAL:** 12 months

**DESCRIPTION:** Marine will capture motion media of a scene consisting of but not limited to the following types: forensic, mishap, crime and tactical/sensitive sites.

**MOS PERFORMING:** 4671

**GRADES:** PVT, PFC, LCPL, CPL, SGT, SSGT

**INITIAL TRAINING SETTING:** FORMAL

**CONDITION:** Given a video acquisition kit and a requirement.

**STANDARD:** Acquiring motion media that focuses on the identifying details of a site and meets the requirement.

**PERFORMANCE STEPS:**
1. Review requirement.
2. Select required equipment.
3. Acclimatize equipment for weather conditions.
4. Conduct equipment operations check.
5. Coordinate with investigative representative/on scene commander for access to site and imagery requirements.
6. Select camera/lighting settings.
7. Document establishing shot of site at multiple angles.
8. Document site in panoramic covering 360 degrees (outside to inside).

9. Document detailed evidence established by investigating official with ruler or other object in site to determine scale.
10. Gather caption data.
11. Caption motion media; as required.
12. Label motion media in accordance with classification guidance from investigating official.
13. Establish chain of custody; as required.
14. Archive motion media; as required.

**REFERENCES:**
1. DOD Captioning Style Guide
2. DODD 5230.9 Clearance of DoD Information for Public Release
3. JCS PUB 1-02 DoD Dictionary of Military and Associated Terms
4. Operator's Manual Operator's Manual
5. SOP Standard Operating Procedures (SOP)

**MISCELLANEOUS:**

**ADMINISTRATIVE INSTRUCTIONS:** Sensitive site examples are enemy weapon caches, mass graves, torture chambers, POW sites, WMD sites, Improvised Explosive Device (IED) sites, enemy use of protected sites (hospitals, religious buildings, schools etc.) Examples of forensic motion media include autopsy, aircraft mishap, vehicle mishap, suicide, material deficiency reports, crime scene etc. Examples of scale may include any common item (ruler, pen, ID card, boot, person) that is placed near or next to item being captured for reference of size. Specialized equipment consists of filters, lighting, color scale, and slate. Do not erase any motion media acquired in support of an official investigation.

---

**4671-VIDS-1008:** Develop motion media products

**EVALUATION-CODED:** NO          **SUSTAINMENT INTERVAL:** 12 months

**DESCRIPTION:** Marine will develop products including, but not limited to: Long form story/production (2-10 minutes), short form story/production ((less than 2 minutes), field production, prime cuts, audio recordings, studio production and training productions. Products can be made available in all formats.

**MOS PERFORMING:** 4671

**GRADES:** PVT, PFC, LCPL, CPL, SGT, SSGT

**INITIAL TRAINING SETTING:** FORMAL

**CONDITION:** In a field environment, given a Tactical Imagery Production System (TIPS), a production workstation, associated software, production equipment, and an operational requirement.

**STANDARD:** Creating a product that meets the operational requirement.

**PERFORMANCE STEPS:**
1. Validate customer requirement.

2. Log in job order.
3. Compile media necessary to complete product.
4. Assemble product.
5. Conduct operations/Quality Control check on product.
6. Submit to COMCAM/Production Chief for approval.
7. Contact requester for approval.
8. Make product modifications; as required.
9. Submit finished product to requestor.
10. Archive finished product.
11. Complete job order.

**REFERENCES:**
1. MCO 3104.1_ Marine Corps Combat Camera Program
2. SOP Standard Operating Procedures (SOP)
3. TIPS Manual Tactical Imagery Production System (TIPS) Training Manual
4. TM 10-5411-200-14 Shelter, Tactical, Expandable, Two-Sided (Tactical Imagery Production System)
5. TM 11084A-OI Environmental Control Unit

**MISCELLANEOUS:**

**ADMINISTRATIVE INSTRUCTIONS:** Multimedia products can include, but are not limited to: command information products in support of information operations, PowerPoint for briefs and/or presentations, computer based training/dvd/vcd/mpg/windows media/real video webpage.

---

**4671-VIDS-1009:** Operate production equipment

**EVALUATION-CODED:** NO          **SUSTAINMENT INTERVAL:** 6 months

**DESCRIPTION:** Marine will operate production equipment including, but not limited to the following: Production workstations, printers, digital media reproduction devices, scanners, video decks and media hard drives.

**MOS PERFORMING:** 4671

**GRADES:** PVT, PFC, LCPL, CPL, SGT, SSGT

**INITIAL TRAINING SETTING:** FORMAL

**CONDITION:** In a field environment, with the aid of references, given a Tactical Imagery Production System (TIPS), production equipment, a production workstation, and associated software.

**STANDARD:** Producing motion media products that meet quality control standards.

**PERFORMANCE STEPS:**
1. Select appropriate equipment needed to accomplish task.
2. Conduct operations check on production equipment.
3. Perform color management.
4. Conduct post operating procedures on production equipment.
5. Perform preventive maintenance as required.

REFERENCES:
1.  MCO 3104.1_ Marine Corps Combat Camera Program
2.  MCWP 3-33.7 Combat Camera in the MAGTF
3.  SOP Standard Operating Procedures (SOP)
4.  TM Technical Manuals
5.  TPH Television Production Handbook, Current Edition, Zettl, Herbert

---

**4671-VIDS-1010:** Create a motion media digital portfolio

**EVALUATION-CODED:** NO          **SUSTAINMENT INTERVAL:** 12 months

**MOS PERFORMING:** 4671

**GRADES:** PVT, PFC, LCPL

**INITIAL TRAINING SETTING:** FORMAL

**CONDITION:** Using motion media, a production workstation, and associated software.

**STANDARD:** Producing a portfolio in accordance with Marine Corps Combat Camera Program.

**PERFORMANCE STEPS:**
1.  Retrieve developed products.
2.  Create portfolio inventory sheet.
3.  Create digital media disc.

**REFERENCES:**
1.  MCO 3104.1_ Marine Corps Combat Camera Program

---

**4671-VIDS-1011:** Conduct motion media pre-production

**EVALUATION-CODED:** NO          **SUSTAINMENT INTERVAL:** 12 months

**DESCRIPTION:** Marine will perform the pre-production process.

**MOS PERFORMING:** 4671

**GRADES:** PVT, PFC, LCPL, CPL, SGT, SSGT

**INITIAL TRAINING SETTING:** FORMAL

**CONDITION:** Given a requirement, a production workstation and associated software, and a DD Form 1995.

**STANDARD:** Resulting in a final approval of the preproduction process.

**PERFORMANCE STEPS:**
1.  Validate requirement.

2. Obtain Production Identification Number (PIN) or Production Approval Number (PAN).
3. Create job order.
4. Coordinate with requestor to develop a script.
5. Write script.
6. Survey locations.
7. Create storyboard.
8. Determine required resources.
9. Conduct final coordination with requestor.
10. Finalize script.
11. Create shooting schedule.

**REFERENCES:**
1. MCO 3104.1_ Marine Corps Combat Camera Program
2. SOP Standard Operating Procedures (SOP)
3. TM Technical Manuals

**MISCELLANEOUS:**

   **ADMINISTRATIVE INSTRUCTIONS:** Operational support includes, but is not limited to: IO, BDA, CMO, HumOps, Intel, MISO, PA, Forensics

---

**4671-VIDS-1012:** Conduct a motion media production

**EVALUATION-CODED:** NO          **SUSTAINMENT INTERVAL:** 12 months

**DESCRIPTION:** Marine will perform the production process.

**MOS PERFORMING:** 4671

**GRADES:** PVT, PFC, LCPL, CPL, SGT, SSGT

**INITIAL TRAINING SETTING:** FORMAL

**CONDITION:** Given a requirement, preproduction documentation, a production workstation and associated software, and production equipment.

**STANDARD:** Resulting in the acquisition of motion media that satisfies the requirement.

**PERFORMANCE STEPS:**
1. Review preproduction documentation.
2. Gather resources.
3. Conduct equipment operations check.
4. Prepare location.
5. Acquire motion media.
6. Validate motion media meets requirements.
7. Consolidate all media required for post production.

**REFERENCES:**
1. DODI 5040.7 Visual Information (VI) Production Procedures
2. MCO 3104.1_ Marine Corps Combat Camera Program
3. SOP Standard Operating Procedures (SOP)

4.  TM Technical Manuals
5.  TPH Television Production Handbook, Current Edition, Zettl, Herbert

---

**4671-VIDS-1013**:  Conduct motion media post-production

**EVALUATION-CODED**:  NO          **SUSTAINMENT INTERVAL**:  12 months

**DESCRIPTION**:  Marine will perform the post-production process.

**MOS PERFORMING**:  4671

**GRADES**:  PVT, PFC, LCPL, CPL, SGT, SSGT

**INITIAL TRAINING SETTING**:  FORMAL

**CONDITION**:  Given a requirement, pre-production documentation, a production workstation, associated software, production equipment and all associated media.

**STANDARD**:  Resulting in the completion of a motion media production that satisfies the requirement.

**PERFORMANCE STEPS**:
1.  Ensure production includes PIN/PAN number.
2.  Import all related media into production workstation.
3.  Create digital graphics and effects; as required.
4.  Edit motion media production.
5.  Submit edited production for quality control.
6.  Make modifications; as required.
7.  Export production to digital media.
8.  Submit motion media production to requestor.
9.  Archive motion media production.
10. Review preproduction documentation and all related media.
11. Complete job order.

**REFERENCES**:
1.  DoD Instruction 5040.7 Visual Information (VI) Production Procedures
2.  MCO 3104.1_ Marine Corps Combat Camera Program
3.  SOP Standard Operating Procedures (SOP)
4.  TM Technical Manuals
5.  TPH Television Production Handbook, Current Edition, Zettl, Herbert

**MISCELLANEOUS**:

  **ADMINISTRATIVE INSTRUCTIONS**:  Training must be in line with current techniques and industry standards, multi-media modeling and motion based graphics, animations, and effects.

---

**7004. 2000-LEVEL EVENTS**

**4671-VIDS-2001:** Maintain motion media equipment

**EVALUATION-CODED:** NO          **SUSTAINMENT INTERVAL:** 12 months

**DESCRIPTION:** Marine will ensure that functional inspections are conducted on a regular basis in order to ensure equipment is combat ready.  Motion media equipment includes, but is not limited to the following:  Production workstations, digital media reproduction devices, scanners, video decks and media hard drives.

**MOS PERFORMING:** 4671

**GRADES:** PVT, PFC, LCPL, CPL, SGT, SSGT

**INITIAL TRAINING SETTING:** MOJT

**CONDITION:** Given video equipment, trouble shooting log and maintenance tools.

**STANDARD:** Ensuring all systems are operational.

**PERFORMANCE STEPS:**
1.  Conduct operations check on systems.
2.  Troubleshoot errors.
3.  Correct error/malfunction.
4.  Identify unserviceable equipment and or components.
5.  Take corrective measures to repair or replace.
6.  Maintain preventative maintenance jacket.

**REFERENCES:**
1.  SOP Standard Operating Procedures (SOP)
2.  TM Technical Manuals

---

**4671-VIDS-2002:** Maintain a motion media portfolio

**EVALUATION-CODED:** NO          **SUSTAINMENT INTERVAL:** 12 months

**MOS PERFORMING:** 4671

**GRADES:** PVT, PFC, LCPL, CPL, SGT, SSGT

**INITIAL TRAINING SETTING:** MOJT

**CONDITION:** With the aid of references, given captured motion media, production equipment, production workstation, and associated software.

**STANDARD:** Maintaining a portfolio in accordance with Marine Corps Combat Camera Program.

**PERFORMANCE STEPS:**
1.  Update COMCAM products.

2. Update portfolio inventory sheet.
3. Create digital media disc.

REFERENCES:
1. MCO 3104.1_ Marine Corps Combat Camera Program
2. MCWP 3-33.7 Combat Camera in the MAGTF
3. SOP Standard Operating Procedures (SOP)

---

**4671-VIDS-2003**:  Conduct a COMCAM capabilities brief

EVALUATION-CODED:  NO          SUSTAINMENT INTERVAL:  12 months

DESCRIPTION:  Marine will conduct a COMCAM Capabilities Brief in order to educate target audience on the capabilities and limitations of Marine Combat Camera which will assist in the proper employment of COMCAM assets.

MOS PERFORMING:  4671

GRADES:  SSGT

INITIAL TRAINING SETTING:  FORMAL

CONDITION:  Given a requirement, a production work station, briefing format, briefing materials, and a target audience.

STANDARD:  Ensuring COMCAM capabilities and limitations are fully explained, within the time allotted and in accordance with Marine Corps Combat Camera Program.

PERFORMANCE STEPS:
1. Review the references.
2. Prepare the brief.
3. Prepare handouts; as required.
4. Rehearse the brief.
5. Conduct the brief.
6. Answer questions.

REFERENCES:
1. MCO 3104.1_ Marine Corps Combat Camera Program
2. MCWP 3-33.7 Combat Camera in the MAGTF
3. SOP Standard Operating Procedures (SOP)

---

COMCAM T&R MANUAL

CHAPTER 8

MOS 4691 INDIVIDUAL EVENTS

CHAPTER 8

MOS 4691 INDIVIDUAL EVENTS

**8000. PURPOSE.** This chapter details the individual events that pertain to MOS 4691, Combat Camera Chief. These events are linked to a service-level Mission Essential Tasks (MET). This linkage tailor's individual training for the selected MET. Each individual event provides an event title, along with the conditions events will be performed under, and the standard to which the event must be performed to be successful.

**8001. EVENT CODING.** Events in this T&R Manual are depicted with an up to 12-character, 3-field alphanumeric system, i.e. XXXX-XXXX-XXXX. This chapter utilizes the following methodology:

a. Field one. This field represents the community. This chapter contains the following community codes:

| Code | Description |
|------|-------------|
| 4691 | Combat Camera Chief |

b. Field two. This field represents the functional/duty area. This chapter contains the following functional/duty areas:

| Code | Description |
|------|-------------|
| MGMT | Management |
| PLAN | Planning |

c. Field three. This field provides the level at which the event is accomplished and numerical sequencing of events. This chapter contains the following event levels:

| Code | Description |
|------|-------------|
| 2000 | Core Plus Skills |

8002. INDEX OF INDIVIDUAL EVENTS

| Event Code | Event | Page |
|---|---|---|
| | MANAGEMENT | |
| 4691-MNGT-2001 | Manage COMCAM unit training plan | 8-4 |
| 4691-MNGT-2002 | Administer COMCAM Standard Operating Procedures | 8-4 |
| 4691-MNGT-2003 | Draft Appendix 9, Annex C to an Operations Order | 8-5 |
| 4691-MNGT-2004 | Develop imagery transmission plan | 8-6 |
| 4691-MNGT-2005 | Submit lessons learned | 8-6 |
| 4691-MNGT-2006 | Supervise the employment of COMCAM equipment | 8-7 |
| 4691-MNGT-2007 | Manage imagery | 8-8 |
| | PLANNING | |
| 4691-PLAN-2008 | Manage the embarkation of COMCAM equipment | 8-8 |
| 4691-PLAN-2009 | Conduct a COMCAM capabilities brief | 8-9 |

8003. 2000-LEVEL EVENTS

**4691-MNGT-2001:** Manage COMCAM unit training plan

**EVALUATION-CODED:** NO          **SUSTAINMENT INTERVAL:** 12 months

**DESCRIPTION:** Marine will manage a Combat Camera unit training plan ensuring that all Marines complete required annual, MOS and unit training requirements.

**MOS PERFORMING:** 4691

**GRADES:** GYSGT, MSGT, MGYSGT

**INITIAL TRAINING SETTING:** MOJT

**CONDITION:** Given the unit and section annual training plans.

**STANDARD:** Ensuring adherence to Marine, MOS and unit training, in accordance with Unit Training Management Guide.

**PERFORMANCE STEPS:**
1. Review HHQ unit training plan.
2. Review unit training plan.
3. Determine training deficiencies.
4. Schedule personnel for training.
5. Update training plan.
6. Submit training plan to higher.

**REFERENCES:**
1. FAC Combat Camera Functional Area Checklist
2. MCO 1553.3A Unit Training Management (UTM)
3. MCRP 3-0A Unit Training Management Guide
4. MCRP 3-0B How to Conduct Training
5. SOP Standard Operating Procedures (SOP)

---

**4691-MNGT-2002:** Administer COMCAM Standard Operating Procedures

**EVALUATION-CODED:** NO          **SUSTAINMENT INTERVAL:** 12 months

**DESCRIPTION:** Marine will ensure policy, standard operating procedures, and desktop procedures are enforced.

**MOS PERFORMING:** 4691

**GRADES:** GYSGT, MSGT, MGYSGT

**INITIAL TRAINING SETTING:** MOJT

**CONDITION:** Given policy, standard operating procedures, and desktop procedures.

**STANDARD**: Ensuring all procedures are followed and discrepancies corrected in accordance with the references.

**PERFORMANCE STEPS**:
1. Review current SOP.
2. Conduct SOP training.
3. Conduct internal inspections.
4. Identify discrepancies.
5. Take corrective action.
6. Recommend updates to SOPs; as appropriate.

**REFERENCES**:
1. MCO 3104.1_ Marine Corps Combat Camera Program
2. SOP Standard Operating Procedures (SOP)

---

**4691-MNGT-2003**: Draft Appendix 9, Annex C to an Operations Order

**EVALUATION-CODED**: NO          **SUSTAINMENT INTERVAL**: 12 months

**DESCRIPTION**: Marine will draft Appendix 9, Annex C to an Operation Order for submission to the COMCAM Officer.

**MOS PERFORMING**: 4691

**GRADES**: GYSGT, MSGT, MGYSGT

**INITIAL TRAINING SETTING**: FORMAL

**CONDITION**: Given an operations plan, Appendix 9, Annex C template, and computer workstation.

**STANDARD**: In a timeline established by the commander in accordance with the Marine Corps Planning Process.

**PERFORMANCE STEPS**:
1. Review operations plan.
2. Identify COMCAM assets.
3. Identify COMCAM functions.
4. Identify COMCAM responsibilities.
5. Identify COMCAM command structure.
6. Identify COMCAM reporting procedures.
7. Identify COMCAM planned employment.
8. Identify COMCAM coordinating instructions.
9. Identify COMCAM related operational parameters.
10. Draft Appendix 9, Annex C.
11. Submit draft to higher.

**REFERENCES**:
1. JCS PUB 1-02 DoD Dictionary of Military and Associated Terms
2. MCWP 3-33.7 Combat Camera in the MAGTF
3. MCWP 5-1 Marine Corps Planning Process (MCPP)
4. NAVMC/MCO 3000.18 Marine Corps Planner's Manual

---

**4691-MNGT-2004:** Develop imagery transmission plan

**EVALUATION-CODED:** NO          **SUSTAINMENT INTERVAL:** 12 months

**DESCRIPTION:** Manage imagery transmission plan and supervise the execution phase. The imagery transmission plan includes but is not limited to the following: NIPR, SIPR, Secure FTP, FFT and other transmission capabilities.

**MOS PERFORMING:** 4691

**GRADES:** GYSGT, MSGT, MGYSGT

**INITIAL TRAINING SETTING:** MOJT

**CONDITION:** Given the operational plan, a requirement to transmit, and communication equipment.

**STANDARD:** Enabling the transmission of imagery to internal and external agencies.

**PERFORMANCE STEPS:**
1. Make liaison with G/S-6.
2. Determine transmission capability.
3. Identify shortfalls.
4. Request additional capabilities; as required.
5. Draft transmission plan.
6. Submit plan to higher.

**REFERENCES:**
1. DOD 5040 Series
2. MCO 3104.1_ Marine Corps Combat Camera Program
3. MCWP 3-33.7 Combat Camera in the MAGTF
4. SOP Standard Operating Procedures (SOP)

---

**4691-MNGT-2005:** Submit lessons learned

**EVALUATION-CODED:** NO          **SUSTAINMENT INTERVAL:** 12 months

**MOS PERFORMING:** 4691

**GRADES:** GYSGT, MSGT, MGYSGT

**INITIAL TRAINING SETTING:** MOJT

**CONDITION:** With the aid of references, given past combat camera operations, a Marine Corps Center for Lessons Learned account, and a CAC enabled computer.

**STANDARD:** Recording successes and failures, encountered during combat camera operations and as directed by MCCLL representative.

**PERFORMANCE STEPS:**
1. Review combat camera operations.
2. Compile information for lessons learned report.

3. Edit and revise collected data.
4. Enter data into written lessons learned report.
5. Submit lessons learned report to higher.

REFERENCES:
1. MCO 3104.1_ Marine Corps Combat Camera Program
2. MCO 3504.1 Marine Corps Lessons Learned Program (MCCLP) and the Marine Corps Center for Lessons Learned (MCCLL)
3. SECNAVINST 5216.5 Naval Correspondence Manual
4. SOP Standard Operating Procedures (SOP)

---

**4691-MNGT-2006:** Supervise the employment of COMCAM equipment

EVALUATION-CODED: NO          SUSTAINMENT INTERVAL: 12 months

MOS PERFORMING: 4691

GRADES: GYSGT, MSGT, MGYSGT

INITIAL TRAINING SETTING: MOJT

CONDITION: Given a mission and equipment.

STANDARD: Supporting operational requirements, in a timeline established by the Standard Operating Procedures (SOP).

PERFORMANCE STEPS:
1. Review mission requirements.
2. Select appropriate equipment needed to accomplish mission.
3. Coordinate required support with appropriate units (Communications, Engineers, Force Protection); as required.
4. Ensure operations checks are conducted.
5. Supervise equipment setup; as required.
6. Supervise equipment operation.
7. Ensure preventive maintenance is conducted; as required.
8. Ensure post operating checks are conducted.
9. Implement the equipment life cycle management program.
10. Establish unit PM schedule.
11. Supervise CMR accountability.

REFERENCES:
1. MCO 3104.1_ Marine Corps Combat Camera Program
2. MCWP 3-33.7 Combat Camera in the MAGTF
3. Operator's Manual Operator's Manual
4. SOP Standard Operating Procedures (SOP)

SUPPORT REQUIREMENTS:

UNITS/PERSONNEL: Personnel required for the TIPS; 1341 Generator Mechanic, 1161 Environmental Control Unit Mechanic, 3531 Motor Vehicle Operator, 3521 Organizational Auto Mechanic, 4068 Data Network Technician, 0651 Data Network Specialist, 0656 Tactical Network Specialist

---

**4691-MNGT-2007**: Manage imagery

**EVALUATION-CODED**: NO      **SUSTAINMENT INTERVAL**: 12 months

**DESCRIPTION**: Manage the accessions process to include initial review, transmission, and receipt of products. During review, the following items will be verified: Product content, metadata, DD Form 2537 and transmissions log.

**MOS PERFORMING**: 4691

**GRADES**: GYSGT, MSGT, MGYSGT

**INITIAL TRAINING SETTING**: MOJT

**CONDITION**: Given a requirement, products, a transmission log, a production workstation and associated software.

**STANDARD**: Ensuring products are accessioned monthly.

**PERFORMANCE STEPS**:
1. Review products.
2. Determine product modifications required.
3. Ensure modifications are made; as required.
4. Select products requiring accession.
5. Supervise the transmission of products.
6. Confirm receipt of products.
7. Review transmission log.

**REFERENCES**:
1. DOD Captioning Style Guide
2. DOD 5040 Series
3. MCO 3104.1_ Marine Corps Combat Camera Program
4. SOP Standard Operating Procedures (SOP)

---

**4691-PLAN-2008**: Manage the embarkation of COMCAM equipment

**EVALUATION-CODED**: NO      **SUSTAINMENT INTERVAL**: 12 months

**DESCRIPTION**: Manage embarkation and coordinate requirements with the S/G-4.

**MOS PERFORMING**: 4691

**GRADES**: GYSGT, MSGT, MGYSGT

**INITIAL TRAINING SETTING**: MOJT

**CONDITION**: Given a mission and assets.

**STANDARD**: Within a timeline established by HHQ S/G-4.

**PERFORMANCE STEPS**:
1. Identify assets required to support mission requirements.

2. Coordinate with command embarkation representatives (S/G-4).
3. Submit TPFDD on Combat Camera assets.
4. Coordinate packing of assets.
5. Coordinate loading of equipment in containers.
6. Coordinate receipt of equipment.
7. Conduct equipment inspection/accountability.

**REFERENCES:**
1. MCO 3104.1_ Marine Corps Combat Camera Program
2. SOP Standard Operating Procedures (SOP)
3. Higher Headquarters OpOrd

---

**4691-PLAN-2009:** Conduct a COMCAM capabilities brief

**EVALUATION-CODED:** NO          **SUSTAINMENT INTERVAL:** 12 months

**DESCRIPTION:** Marine will conduct a COMCAM Capabilities Brief in order to educate target audience on the capabilities and limitations of Marine Combat Camera which will assist in the proper employment of COMCAM assets.

**MOS PERFORMING:** 4691

**GRADES:** GYSGT, MSGT, MGYSGT

**INITIAL TRAINING SETTING:** FORMAL

**CONDITION:** Given a requirement, a production work station, briefing format, briefing materials, and a target audience.

**STANDARD:** Ensuring COMCAM capabilities and limitations are fully explained in accordance with MCO 3104.1AB Marine Corps Combat Camera Program.

**PERFORMANCE STEPS:**
1. Review the references.
2. Prepare the brief.
3. Prepare handouts; as required.
4. Rehearse the brief.
5. Conduct the brief.
6. Answer questions.

**REFERENCES:**
1. MCO 3104.1_ Marine Corps Combat Camera Program
2. MCWP 3-33.7 Combat Camera in the MAGTF
3. SOP Standard Operating Procedures (SOP)

---

COMCAM T&R MANUAL

APPENDIX A

ACRONYMS AND ABBREVIATIONS

CMCC . . . . . . . . . . . . . . . . . . . . . . Classified Material Control Center
CMR . . . . . . . . . . . . . . . . . . . . . . . Consolidated Memorandum Report
COMCAM . . . . . . . . . . . . . . . . . . . . . . . . . . . . . . . Combat Camera
COMSEC . . . . . . . . . . . . . . . . . . . . . . . . . Communications Security
CONOPS . . . . . . . . . . . . . . . . . . . . . . . . . . Contingency Operations
COTS . . . . . . . . . . . . . . . . . . . . . . . . . . Commercial Off The Shelf
CSAS . . . . . . . . . . . . . . . . . . . . . . . Combat Still Acquisition System
CVAS . . . . . . . . . . . . . . . . . . . . . . Combat Video Acquisition System
DoD . . . . . . . . . . . . . . . . . . . . . . . . . . . . Department of Defense
DoDD . . . . . . . . . . . . . . . . . . . . . . . Department of Defense Directive
DoDI . . . . . . . . . . . . . . . . . . . . . . Department of Defense Instruction
DRRS . . . . . . . . . . . . . . . . . . . . . Defense Readiness Reporting System
FM . . . . . . . . . . . . . . . . . . . . . . . . . . . . . . Field Manual (army)
GOTS . . . . . . . . . . . . . . . . . . . . . . . . . . . Government Off the Shelf
JCS . . . . . . . . . . . . . . . . . . . . . . . . . . . . . Joint Chiefs of Staff
JP . . . . . . . . . . . . . . . . . . . . . . . . . . . . . . . Joint Publication
MAGTF . . . . . . . . . . . . . . . . . . . . . . . . Marine Air-Ground Task Force
MCLL . . . . . . . . . . . . . . . . . . . . . . . . . Marine Corps Lessons Learned
MCPP . . . . . . . . . . . . . . . . . . . . . . . . Marine Corps Planning Process
MCTL . . . . . . . . . . . . . . . . . . . . . . . . . . . Marine Corps Task List
MCWP . . . . . . . . . . . . . . . . . . . . Marine Corps Warfighting Publication
MEF . . . . . . . . . . . . . . . . . . . . . . . . . . Marine Expeditionary Force
MET . . . . . . . . . . . . . . . . . . . . . . . . . . . . . Mission Essential Task
METL . . . . . . . . . . . . . . . . . . . . . . . . Mission Essential Task List
MEU . . . . . . . . . . . . . . . . . . . . . . . . . . Marine Expeditionary Unit
NGO . . . . . . . . . . . . . . . . . . . . . . . . Non-Governmental Organization
OPLAN . . . . . . . . . . . . . . . . . . . . . . . . . . . . . . . Operation Plan
OPORD . . . . . . . . . . . . . . . . . . . . . . . . . . . . . . . Operation Order
OPSEC . . . . . . . . . . . . . . . . . . . . . . . . . . . . Operations Security
OPT . . . . . . . . . . . . . . . . . . . . . . . . . . . Operational Planning Team
PM . . . . . . . . . . . . . . . . . . . . . . . . . . . . Preventative Maintenance
TIPS . . . . . . . . . . . . . . . . . . . . . Tactical Imagery Production System
TPFDD . . . . . . . . . . . . . . . . . . . Time-phased Force and Deployment Data
UNS . . . . . . . . . . . . . . . . . . . . . . . . . . . . Universal Need Statement
UTM . . . . . . . . . . . . . . . . . . . . . . . . . . . . Unit Training Management
VIIES . . . . . . . . . . . . . . . . Visual Information Imagery Editing System
VIRIN . . . . . . . . . . . . . Visual Information Record Identification Number

COMCAM T&R MANUAL

APPENDIX B

TERMS AND DEFINITIONS

Terms in this glossary are subject to change as applicable orders and directives are revised. Terms established by Marine Corps orders or directives take precedence after definitions found in Joint Pub 1-02, *DOD Dictionary of Military and Associated Terms*.

A

**After Action Review.** A professional discussion of training events conducted after all training to promote learning among training participants. The formality and scope increase with the command level and size of the training evolution. For longer exercises, they should be planned for at predetermined times during an exercise. The results of the AAR shall be recorded on an after action report and forwarded to higher headquarters. The commander and higher headquarters use the results of an AAR to reallocate resources, reprioritize their training plan, and plan for future training.

**Assessment.** An assessment is an informal judgment of the unit's proficiency and resources made by a commander or trainer to gain insight into the unit's overall condition. It serves as the basis for the midrange plan. Commanders make frequent use of these determinations during the course of the combat readiness cycle in order to adjust, prioritize or modify training events and plans.

C

**Chaining.** Chaining is a process that enables unit leaders to effectively identify subordinate collective events and individual events that support a specific collective event. For example, collective training events at the 4000-level are directly supported by collective events at the 3000-level. Utilizing the building block approach to progressive training, these collective events are further supported by individual training events at the 1000 and 2000-levels. When a higher-level event by its nature requires the completion of lower level events, they are "chained"; Sustainment credit is given for all lower level events chained to a higher event.

**Collective Event.** A collective event is a clearly defined, discrete, and measurable activity, action, or event (i.e., task) that requires organized team or unit performance and leads to accomplishment of a mission or function. A collective task is derived from unit missions or higher-level collective tasks. Task accomplishment requires performance of procedures composed of supporting collective or individual tasks. A collective task describes the exact performance a group must perform in the field under actual operational conditions. The term "collective" does not necessarily infer that a unit accomplishes the event. A unit, such as a squad or platoon conducting an attack; may accomplish a collective event or, it may be accomplished by an individual to accomplish a unit mission, such as a battalion supply officer completing a reconciliation of the battalion's CMR.

Thus, many collective events will have titles that are the same as individual events; however, the standard and condition will be different because the scope of the collective event is broader.

**Collective Training Standards (CTS).** Criteria that specify mission and functional area unit proficiency standards for combat, combat support, and combat service support units. They include tasks, conditions, standards, evaluator instruction, and key indicators. CTS are found within collective training events in T&R Manuals.

**Combat Readiness Cycle.** The combat readiness cycle depicts the relationships within the building block approach to training. The combat readiness cycle progresses from T&R Manual individual core skills training, to the accomplishment of collective training events, and finally, to a unit's participation in a contingency or actual combat. The combat readiness cycle demonstrates the relationship of core capabilities to unit combat readiness. Individual core skills training and the training of collective events lead to proficiency and the ability to accomplish the unit's stated mission.

**Combat Readiness Percentage (CRP).** The CRP is a quantitative numerical value used in calculating collective training readiness based on the E-Coded events that support the unit METL. CRP is a concise measure of unit training accomplishments. This numerical value is only a snapshot of training readiness at a specific time. As training is conducted, unit CRP will continuously change.

**Component Events.** Component events are the major tasks involved in accomplishing a collective event. Listing these tasks guide Marines toward the accomplishment of the event and help evaluators determine if the task has been done to standard. These events may be lower-level collective or individual events that must be accomplished.

**Condition.** The condition describes the training situation or environment under which the training event or task will take place. Expands on the information in the title by identifying when, where and why the event or task will occur and what materials, personnel, equipment, environmental provisions, and safety constraints must be present to perform the event or task in a real-world environment. Commanders can modify the conditions of the event to best prepare their Marines to accomplish the assigned mission (e.g. in a desert environment; in a mountain environment; etc.).

**Core Competency.** Core competency is the comprehensive measure of a unit's ability to accomplish its assigned MET. It serves as the foundation of the T&R Program. Core competencies are those unit core capabilities and individual core skills that support the commander's METL and T/O mission statement. Individual competency is exhibited through demonstration of proficiency in specified core tasks and core plus tasks. Unit proficiency is measured through collective tasks.

**Core Capabilities.** Core capabilities are the essential functions a unit must be capable of performing during extended contingency/combat operations. Core unit capabilities are based upon mission essential tasks derived from operational plans; doctrine and established tactics; techniques and procedures.

**Core Plus Capabilities.** Core plus capabilities are advanced capabilities that are environment, mission, or theater specific. Core plus capabilities may entail high-risk, high-cost training for missions that are less likely to be assigned in combat.

**Core Plus Skills.** Core plus skills are those advanced skills that are environment, mission, rank, or billet specific. 2000-level training is designed to make Marines proficient in core skills in a specific billet or at a specified rank at the Combat Ready level. 3000-8000-level training produces combat leaders and fully qualified section members at the Combat Qualified level. Marines trained at the Combat Qualified level are those the commanding officer feels are capable of accomplishing unit-level missions and of directing the actions of subordinates. Many core plus tasks are learned via MOJT, while others form the base for curriculum in career level MOS courses taught by the formal school.

**Core Skills.** Core skills are those essential basic skills that "make" a Marine and qualify that Marine for an MOS. They are the 1000-level skills introduced in entry-level training at formal schools.

D

**Defense Readiness Reporting System (DRRS).** A comprehensive readiness reporting system that evaluates readiness on the basis of the actual missions and capabilities assigned to the forces. It is a capabilities-based, adaptive, near real-time reporting system for the entire Department of Defense.

**Deferred Event.** A T&R event that a commanding officer may postpone when in his or her judgment, a lack of logistic support, ammo, ranges, or other training assets requires a temporary exemption. CRP cannot be accrued for deferred "E-Coded" events.

**Delinquent Event.** An event becomes delinquent when a Marine or unit exceeds the sustainment interval for that particular event. The individual or unit must update the delinquent event by first performing all prerequisite events. When the unit commander deems that performing all prerequisite is unattainable, then the delinquent event will be re-demonstrated under the supervision of the appropriate evaluation authority.

E

**E-coded Event.** An "E-Coded" event is a collective T&R event that is a noted indicator of capability or, a noted Collective skill that contributes to the unit's ability to perform the supported MET. As such, only "E-Coded" events are assigned a CRP value and used to calculate a unit's CRP.

**Entry-level training.** Pipeline training that equips students for service with the Marine Operating Forces.

**Evaluation.** Evaluation is a continuous process that occurs at all echelons, during every phase of training and can be both formal and informal. Evaluations ensure that Marines and units are capable of conducting their combat mission. Evaluation results are used to reallocate resources, reprioritize the training plan, and plan for future training.

**Event (Training).** (1) An event is a significant training occurrence that is identified, expanded and used as a building block and potential milestone for a unit's training. An event may include formal evaluations. (2) An event within the T&R Program can be an individual training evolution, a collective training evolution or both. Through T&R events, the unit commander ensures that individual Marines and the unit progress from a combat capable status to a Fully Combat Qualified (FCQ) status.

**Event Component.** Event components are the major procedures (i.e., actions) that must occur to perform a Collective Event to standard.

**Exercise Commander (EC).** The Commanding General, Marine Expeditionary Force or his appointee will fill this role, unless authority is delegated to the respective commander of the Division, Wing, or FSSG. Responsibilities and functions of the EC include: (1) designate unit(s) to be evaluated, (2) may designate an exercise director, (3) prescribe exercise objectives and T&R events to be evaluated, (4) coordinate with commands or agencies external to the Marine Corps and adjacent Marine Corps commands, when required.

**Exercise Director (ED).** Designated by the EC to prepare, conduct, and report all evaluation results. Responsibilities and functions of the ED include: (1) Publish a letter of instruction (LOI) that: delineates the T&R events to be evaluated, establishes timeframe of the exercise, lists responsibilities of various elements participating in the exercise, establishes safety requirements/guidelines, and lists coordinating instructions. (2) Designate the TEC and TECG to operate as the central control agency for the exercise. (3) Assign evaluators, to include the senior evaluator, and ensure that those evaluators are properly trained. (4) Develop the general exercise scenario taking into account any objectives/events prescribed by the EC. (5) Arrange for all resources to include: training areas, airspace, aggressor forces, and other required support.

I

**Individual Readiness.** The individual training readiness of each Marine is measured by the number of individual events required and completed for the rank or billet currently held.

**Individual Training.** Training that applies to individual Marines. Examples include rifle qualifications and HMMWV driver licensing.

**Individual Training Standards (ITS).** Individual Training Standards specify training tasks and standards for each MOS or specialty within the Marine Corps. In most cases, once an MOS or community develops a T&R, the ITS order will be cancelled. However, most communities will probably fold a large portion of their ITS into their new T&R Manual.

M

**Marine Corps Ground Training and Readiness (T&R) Program.** The T&R Program is the Marine Corps' primary tool for planning and conducting training, for planning and conducting training evaluation, and for assessing training readiness. The program will provide the commander with standardized programs of instruction for units within the ground combat, combat support, and combat service support communities. It consolidates the ITS, CTS, METL and other individual and unit training management tools.  T&R is a program of standards that systematizes commonly accepted skills, is open to innovative change, and above all, tailors the training effort to the unit's mission.  Further, T&R serves as a training guide and provides commanders an immediate assessment of unit combat readiness by assigning a CRP to key training events.  In short, the T&R Program is a building block approach to training that maximizes flexibility and produces the best-trained Marines possible.

**Mission Essential Task(s) MET(s).**  A MET is a collective task in which an organization must be proficient in order to accomplish an appropriate portion of its wartime mission(s).  MET listings are the foundation for the T&R Manual; all events in the T&R Manual support a MET.

**Mission Essential Task List (METL).**  Descriptive training document that provides units a clear, war fighting focused description of collective actions necessary to achieve wartime mission proficiency.  The service-level METL, that which is used as the foundation of the T&R Manual, is developed using Marine Corps doctrine, Operational Plans, T/Os, UJTL, UNTL, and MCTL. For community based T&R Manuals, an occupational field METL is developed to focus the community's collective training standards. Commanders develop their unit METL from the service-level METL, operational plans, contingency plans, and SOPs.

O

**Operational Readiness (DOD, NATO).**  OR is the capability of a unit/formation, ship, weapon system, or equipment to perform the missions or functions for which it is organized or designed.  May be used in a general sense or to express a level or degree of readiness.

P

**Performance step.**  Performance steps are included in the components of an Individual T&R Event.  They are the major procedures (i.e., actions) a unit Marine must accomplish to perform an individual event to standard.  They describe the procedure the task performer must take to perform the task under operational conditions and provide sufficient information for a task performer to perform the procedure (May necessitate identification of supporting steps, procedures, or actions in outline form.).  Performance steps follow a logical progression and should be followed sequentially, unless otherwise stated.  Normally, performance steps are listed only for 1000-level individual events (those that are taught in the entry-level MOS school).

**Prerequisite Event.**  Prerequisites are the academic training and/or T&R events that must be completed prior to attempting the event.

R

**Readiness (DOD).**  Readiness is the ability of US military forces to fight and meet the demands of the national military strategy.  Readiness is the synthesis of two distinct but interrelated levels:  (a) Unit readiness--The ability to provide capabilities required by combatant commanders to execute assigned missions.  This is derived from the ability of each unit to deliver the outputs for which it was designed. (b) Joint readiness--The combatant commander's ability to integrate and synchronize ready combat and support forces to execute assigned missions.

S

**Section Skill Tasks.** Section Skills are those competencies directly related to unit functioning. They are group rather than individual in nature, and require participation by a section (S-1, S-2, S-3, etc).

**Simulation Training.** Simulators provide the additional capability to develop and hone core and core plus skills. Accordingly, the development of simulator training events for appropriate T&R syllabi can help maintain valuable combat resources while reducing training time and cost. Therefore, in cases where simulator fidelity and capabilities are such that simulator training closely matches that of actual training events, T&R Manual developers may include the option of using simulators to accomplish the training. CRP credit will be earned for E-coded simulator events based on assessment of relative training event performance.

**Standard.** A standard is a statement that establishes criteria for how well a task or learning objective must be performed. The standard specifies how well, completely, or accurately a process must be performed or product produced. For higher-level collective events, it describes why the event is being done and the desired end-state of the event. Standards become more specific for lower-level events and outline the accuracy, time limits, sequencing, quality, product, process, restrictions, etc., that indicate the minimum acceptable level of performance required of the event. At a minimum, both collective and individual training standards consist of a task, the condition under which the task is to be performed, and the evaluation criteria that will be used to verify that the task has been performed to a satisfactory level.

**Sustainment Training.** Periodic retraining or demonstration of an event required maintaining the minimum acceptable level of proficiency or capability required to accomplish a training objective. Sustainment training goes beyond the entry-level and is designed to maintain or further develop proficiency in a given set of skills.

**Systems Approach to Training (SAT).** An orderly process for analyzing, designing, developing, implementing, and evaluating a unit's training program to ensure the unit, and the Marines of that unit acquire the knowledge and skills essential for the successful conduct of the unit's wartime missions.

T

**Training Task.** This describes a direct training activity that pertains to an individual Marine. A task is composed of 3 major components: a description of what is to be done, a condition, and a standard.

**Technical Exercise Controller (TEC).** The TEC is appointed by the ED, and usually comes from his staff or a subordinate command. The TEC is the senior evaluator within the TECG and should be of equal or higher grade than the commander(s) of the unit(s) being evaluated. The TEC is responsible for ensuring that the evaluation is conducted following the instructions contained in this order and MCO 1553.3B. Specific T&R Manuals are used as the source for evaluation criteria.

**Tactical Exercise Control Group (TECG).** A TECG is formed to provide subject matter experts in the functional areas being evaluated. The benefit of establishing a permanent TECG is to have resident, dedicated evaluation authority experience, and knowledgeable in evaluation technique. The responsibilities and functions of the TECG include: (1) developing a detailed exercise scenario to include the objectives and events prescribed by the EC/ED in the exercise LOI; (2) conducting detailed evaluator training prior to the exercise; (3) coordinating and controlling role players and aggressors; (4) compiling the evaluation data submitted by the evaluators and submitting required results to the ED; (5) preparing and conducting a detailed exercise debrief for the evaluated unit(s).

**Training Plan.** The training plan is a training document that outlines the general plan for the conduct of individual and collective training in an organization for specified periods of time.

**U**

**Unit CRP.** Unit CRP is a percentage of the E-coded collective events that support the unit METL accomplished by the unit. Unit CRP is the average of all MET CRP.

**Unit Evaluation.** All units in the Marine Corps must be evaluated, either formally or informally, to ensure they are capable of conducting their combat mission. Informal evaluations should take place during all training events. The timing of formal evaluations is critical and should, when appropriate, be directly related to the units' operational deployment cycle. Formal evaluations should take place after the unit has been staffed with the majority of its personnel, has had sufficient time to train to individual and collective standards, and early enough in the training cycle so there is sufficient time to correctly identified weaknesses prior to deployment. All combat units, and units task organized for combat require formal evaluations prior to operational deployments.

**Unit Training Management (UTM).** Unit training management is the use of the SAT and Marine Corps training principles in a manner that maximizes training results and focuses the training priorities of the unit on its wartime mission. UTM governs the major peacetime training activity of the Marine Corps and applies to all echelons of the Total Force.

**W**

**Waived Event.** An event that is waived by a commanding officer when in his or her judgment, previous experience or related performance satisfies the requirement of a particular event.

APPENDIX C

REFERENCES

**Chairman of the Joint Chiefs of Staff Manual (CJCSM)**
3122.01  Joint Operational Planning And Execution System
3122.03  Joint Operation Planning and Execution System, Volume II (Planning Formats and Guidance)

**Department of the Army Pamphlet (DA PAM)**
25-91  Visual Information Procedures

**Department of Defense (DOD)**
5040.2  Joint Combat Camera Operations
6050.5  Hazardous Material Information System User's Guide

**Department of Defense Directive (DODD)**
5040.2  Visual Information (VI)
5040.3  DoD Joint Visual Information Services
5040.4  Joint Combat Camera (COMCAM) Program
5040.5  Alteration of Official DoD Imagery
5230.9  Clearance of DoD Information for Public Release
5400.7  Freedom of Information Act (FOIA) Program
5160.48  DoD Public Affairs and Visual Information (PA&VI) Education and Training (E&T)

**Department of Defense Instruction (DODI)**
1322.20  Development and Management of Interactive Courseware (ICW) for Military Training
5040.6  Life-cycle Management of DOD Visual Information (VI)
5040.7  Visual Information (VI) Production Procedures

**Fleet Marine Force Manual (FMFM)**
3-53  Psychological Operations

**Joint Chiefs of Staff Publication (JCS PUB)**
1-02  DoD Dictionary of Military and Associated Terms

**Joint Interoperability Engineering Organization Report (JIEO Report)**
8307  DOD Guide to Selecting Computer-Based Multimedia Standards, Technologies, Products and Practices

**Marine Administrative Message (MARADMIN)**
469/05 Use of International Maritime Satellite (INMARSAT)

**Marine Corps Doctrinal Publications (MCDPs)**
5 Planning

**Marine Corps Order (MCO)**
1553.3  Marine Corps Unit Training Management

3093.1  Intraoperability and Interoperability of Marine Corps Tactical C4I Systems
3104.1  VI and COMCAM Support Manual
3430.8  Policy for Information Operations
3440.7  Marine Corps Support to Civil Authorities
4700-15/1  Equipment Record Procedures
4790.2 MIMMS Field Procedures Manual
4790.7 MIMMS AIS Headquarters Users Manual
4860.3  Commercial Activities (CA) Program
5230.18  Clearance of Department of Defense Information for Public Release
5500.13  Physical Security
5510.17  Policy for Handling and Safeguarding North Atlantic Treaty Organization (NATO) Material
5510.9  Security of Information for Public Release
5720.71  Joint Public Affairs Operations
5720.76  Standardization of Publicly Accessible Web Pages
P1610.7  Performance Evaluation System (PES)
P4400.150  Consumer Level Supply
P4400.82  MIMMS Controlled Item Management Manual
P4790.2  MIMMS Field Procedures Manual
P4790.3  MIMMS Depot Policy Manual
P5090.2  Environmental Compliance and Protection Manual
P5090.2  Marine Corps Hazardous Waste Program
P5600.31  Marine Corps Publications and Printing Regulations
P7100.8  Field Budget Guidance Manual

**Marine Corps Reference Publication (MCRP)**
3-0B (FMFM 0-1A)  How to Conduct Training
3-33.7  COMCAM Joint Doctrine

**Marine Corps Warfighting Publications (MCWPs)**
3-33.7  Combat Camera in the MAGTF
5-1  Marine Corps Planning Process

**Navy Marine Corps (NAVMC)**
10245  Equipment Repair Order (ERO)

**Navy Marine Corps Directive (NAVMC DIR)**
3500.54  Combat Camera T&R

**Office of the Chief of Naval Operations Instruction (OPNAVINST)**
3104.1  Naval Visual Information and Combat Camera Program Policy and Responsibilities
3104.3  Naval Combat Camera (COMCAM) Program, Policy, Responsibilities
3501.320  Required Operational Capabilities (ROC)/Projected Operational Environment (POE) for Fleet Imaging Commands (FLTIMAGCOM)
5510.1  Department of the Navy Information and Personnel Security Program Regulation

**Secretary of Navy Instructions (SECNAVINST)**
3104.1  Department of the Navy Visual Information and Combat Camera Program
5216.5  Naval Correspondence Manual
5510.30  Dept of Navy Personnel Security Program
5510.36  Dept of the Navy Information and Personnel Security Program Regulations

**Technical Manuals**
TM 11084A-OI  ECU
TM 10-5411-200-14  Shelter Expandable

**Miscellaneous**
Associated Press Stylebook
Color Confidence by Tim Grey
Digital Color Management by Giorgianni Madden
DMS System Administration Manual
DOD Style Guide
Editing with Avid Xpress Pro and Avid Xpress DV
How to shoot a Movie & Video Story
Local Standing Operating Procedure (SOP)
Photography
Pocket Guide to Color with Digital Applications by Dr. Thomas Schildgen
Operator's Manual
Real World Color Management by Bruce Fraser, Chris Murphy and Fred Bunting
SL-3 Major Components of End Items
System Schematics
Tactical Imagery Production System (TIPS) Training Manual
Television Production Handbook
The Designer's Desktop Manual by Jason Sammons
The Five C's of Cinematography
US Copyright Law Title 17
Video Field Production and Editing